HEALING THE FAMILY WITHIN

By Robert Subby

Health Communications, Inc.
Deerfield Beach, Florida

Library of Congress Cataloging-in-Publication Data

Subby, Robert
     Healing the family within: on the road to recovery/Robert Subby.
        p.   cm.
     ISBN 1-55874-071-6
     1. Co-dependence (Psychology)   2. Co-dependents — Rehabil-
     itation.
I. Title.
RC569.5.C63S82   1990   90-34302
616.86—dc20   CIP

Publisher: Health Communications, Inc.
               3201 S.W. 15th Street
               Deerfield Beach, Florida 33442

Acknowledgments

I would like to thank my colleagues and clients who have helped me over the years to discover the family within. I would especially like to thank my sponsor, Walt H., who helped me recover my family within. Special acknowledgment to Scott Roger Young — thank you for all your technical assistance. And to Donna R. for allowing me to share her story.

"Bob is truly a leader in teaching us about families and change. His straightforward style is both humorous and insightful. In *Healing The Family Within* Bob takes the reader on a unique journey into self-discovery and personal healing. My hope is that everyone might read this book."

— *Terry Kellogg*

Bob Subby is a leading pioneer in the discovery and establishment of co-dependency as a clinical phenomenon. His newest work is also pioneering. This time he leads us towards a true integration and understanding of our family within. I highly recommend this book."

— *John Bradshaw*

Dedication

To my daughter, Sara Page Subby, and to my stepdaughters, Beth, Stephanie and Carrie (Cubbie) Hansen, who have brought me great joy and happiness.

Contents

Figures

PART ONE

I Meet My
Inner Family

So you're a co-dependent. So you're an adult child. So you come from a troubled family. The important question now is where do you go from here. When I asked myself these questions, I discovered that I was lost. I would have panicked, but I'd been lost for so long, the only thing I felt was relief. "If nothing else," I thought to myself, "I know I'm lost."

Knowing this, the choices seemed simple. I could sit and do nothing or I could start trying to find my way out. I asked myself, "How does one who is lost go about getting found?" As I sat and mulled over the possibilities, I recognized that there was a dialogue going on inside my head. It was a fairly abusive conversation, to be sure, but it seemed clear that there were at least three distinct voices: that of an emotional child, a guilt-inducing adult and a shaming parent.

Inner Child: I'm scared! I don't like being lost. Bad things always happen when you're lost.

Inner Adult: Shut up! We don't have time for all your whining. Be a man. Scared is for cowards.

Inner Parent: You'll never amount to anything. You're always getting lost in your feelings. You've been a disappointment since the day you were born. I'm ashamed of you.

Inner Child: It's not my fault we're lost!

Inner Adult: Whose fault is it then? Maybe if you weren't such an emotional cripple we wouldn't be so lost in the first place.

Inner Parent: God helps them who help themselves. As far as I'm concerned, you're beyond help. You should be grateful God doesn't smite you for being such a wretch.

By turning in on this self-defeating dialogue, it became obvious to me that I was my own worst enemy, and that the only place I was lost was inside myself. Like most adult children/co-dependents my biggest problem was the lack of a healthy inner family. More to the point, it was the lack of a healthy inner adult and parent to guide me when things got tough.

So began the process of discovering and healing my family within. This journey was a process of learning to identify the three dimensions of my inner family, helping them to move beyond the co-dependent scripts of their past and reclaiming their personal power. It was about the process of rebuilding my life and recovering from the inside out. It was a journey through which I learned to welcome and embrace my family within.

Out Of Sight, Out Of Mind,
Out Of Body

There I was, standing at the back of the church, trying to prepare myself for the long walk to the altar. Inside the chapel several hundred guests waited patiently for the ceremony to begin.

It was early spring, a time of uncertain weather. The sun was just beginning to set behind the clouds, and I was awed by the brilliant rays of colored light that came streaming through the stained-glass windows. As I stood there watching, it began to rain. Several bolts of lightning struck near the church and the sound of thunder seemed to vibrate inside my body. An icy chill ran up my spine and I was filled with a terrible sense of impending doom.

Inside I was coming unglued. My heart started racing, my ears began to ring, my mouth went dry, and I was having trouble catching my breath. Suddenly I heard a child's voice screaming inside me: *"I don't want to do this! Please don't make me do this! I don't want to get married! I'm too young! I want to go home! I think I'm going to be sick! Get me out of here!"*

Then I heard another voice — scolding, cold and unfeeling: *"For God's sake, man. Pull yourself together and get with the program. You're acting like a child. What's all this 'feeling' crap? Knock it off this instant!*

"This is no time to be having second thoughts. Besides, if we back out now, we'll lose all that earnest money we put down on the new house. And what about that hard-to-get eight percent, fixed-rate 30-year mortgage we've applied for? And what about all the important tax benefits and financial gains we'll miss out on? Have you thought about that?

"Well, just remember, opportunities like these do not happen every day. So, what's it going to be? Are you going to act like a man or not?"

No sooner had this logical assault ended when I heard yet another voice, a shaming parental voice: *"You should be ashamed of yourself, young man! You're nothing but a sniveling little brat, always thinking about yourself. Just once I wish you would try to think about someone other than yourself.*

"You see all those people sitting out there? How do you think they would feel if we backed out now? Why, if you don't go through with this wedding, you will never be able to show your face in town again.

"What in God's name could you be thinking? After all your family has done for you, is this the way you're going to repay them? And what about that poor woman you promised to marry? She deserves better than this.

"I only hope that God will forgive you for what you've been thinking. God knows I am trying to."

Out Of Body, Out Of Mind

Meanwhile back at the church, things were moving right along. The wedding march had started to play — my cue to start down toward the altar. *"One foot in front of the other,"* I told myself. *"Easy does it. That's it, just a few more steps. Don't worry, Bob, everything is going to work out."*

Halfway down the aisle I started feeling dizzy. I thought for sure I was going to pass out. Suddenly, the next thing I knew, I was floating weightless outside of my body. *"What's happening?"* I asked myself. *"I must be having one of those out-of-body experiences. Wow, what a rush!"*

As I drifted over the crowd I looked down and saw myself kneeling at the altar. It was like watching a movie of someone else's wedding. The conversations inside me had stopped and for the first time that day I was feeling no pain.

Unfortunately all good things must come to an end. No sooner had I begun to really enjoy myself when reality struck and I was jerked back into my body. The ceremony was over and all the guests were standing on their feet applauding. *"My God,"* I thought to myself, *"I'm married."*

It wasn't until an hour or so later, when I arrived at my parents' home for the reception and stepped out of the car into the rain, that I began to realize what had happened. I didn't like where my thoughts were headed so I put my mind in neutral, pulled my jacket over my head and made a beeline for the house. Once inside, I headed straight for the bathroom, where I thought I might get some time alone. No such luck. I ran right into my mother. She pulled me aside and asked if I would mind running back out to the car to retrieve some gifts that had been left in the trunk.

"No problem," I replied, and started down the hall toward the back entrance of the house. Still in a daze I grabbed hold of the crescent handle on the storm door and inadvertently managed to hook my wedding ring around the end of it. The next thing I knew I was lying flat on my back. The pain was tremendous, and it took everything I had not to scream out loud. God forbid, I would have allowed myself to do anything as human as that!

As I lay there bleeding from the cut on my finger, with my hand still dangling like a dead fish from the handle of the door and my wedding ring neatly bent into the shape of an egg, it occurred to me that maybe someone was trying to tell me something. Whatever it was, I knew it would not be good. And to make matters worse the dynamic trio inside my head was at it again:

Child: Now what are we going to do?

Parent: Don't ask me.

Adult: Well, I know what I'm going to do. I'm going to pick myself up by the bootstraps, climb back into the saddle and make the best of it.

Child: So it's business as usual, huh?

Adult: That's right, business as usual.

Child: Pip pip, cheerio, popsicle, and all that rot, dontcha know.

Parent: That's right, carry on.

So I pulled myself off the ground, brushed back my hair, straight-
ened my ring, bandaged my wound and returned to the party as
though nothing had happened.

Out Of The Dream, Into The Nightmare

On the outside I must have looked like just another one of those
happy, well-adjusted guys pursuing the Great American Dream —
you know, the perfect marriage, great job, plenty of money, a house
in the 'burbs with a white picket fence and two cars in the garage,
along with a couple of kids (one of each), a loyal dog and ten or 20
really good friends.

Not a bad fantasy for someone who is actually living on this
planet. Unfortunately I was not. No, sir, no fairy tale endings or
happily-ever-afters for me. In fact the story of my first marriage read
more like a Greek tragedy than a love story. Within only three short
years my Great American Dream would end in painful divorce.

Divorce. My worst nightmare. The voices continued: *"How could
I have failed so miserably? Where did I go wrong? Why couldn't I
make it work? If only I had tried a little harder. I should never have
married in the first place. Maybe the truth is that I'm just incapable
of loving anyone."*

If ever I felt lost in the shuffle, it was now. Like it or not, I had
become just another statistic — one of the millions of *Ozzie and
Harriet* fans who grew up believing they would never let divorce
happen to them.

But this was not the first time I had guessed wrong about my
future. Ten years earlier I had made a promise to myself that I was
never going to become an alcoholic, and look where that promise
went. I was beginning to think that I was destined to end up doing
everything I said I would never do.

Perhaps if I had still been a practicing alcoholic during my
marriage, the whole situation might have made more sense to me.
At least then I would have been able to blame everything on my
drinking. But this was not the case. Only three months before
getting married I had celebrated my fourth year of sobriety in
Alcoholics Anonymous (AA) and was well on my way to earning
my black belt in sobriety.

What a laugh. I was about as close to having a black belt in
sobriety as I was to winning the Publisher's Clearinghouse Sweep-
stakes. Crazy as it all seems now, I honestly believed back then
that being sober meant I was ready to handle anything, including

marriage. I told myself that being married was just one of those things you did on the way to becoming a healthy and productive member of society.

Now, however, I see that the root cause of my problems had little to do with the external realities of my life. My alcoholism and my divorce were little more than symptoms of my troubled inner family.

In The Beginning

Seven years ago I was privileged to be one of a small group of helping professionals from around the country who had got together to talk about the emerging subject of adult children. We were more than just a gathering of professionals. With few exceptions we were a group of recovering adult children looking for support — support that we were not crazy, and that we had discovered something important about our lives and the lives of millions of others like us.

As we shared our life stories, it became clear that we were all searching for something beyond whatever our personal and professional experiences in AA, Al-Anon and therapy had taught us about recovering as adult children.

We came away with a deeper understanding of the need to pool our energies and work together in order to advance the cause of adult children. So it was that the idea for the National Association of Children of Alcoholics (NACoA) was first born. In the years since its birth NACoA has grown into an organization with over ten thousand members. More impressive than its membership, however, is the growing number of people who have been helped by its services.

The struggle of those early years with NACoA marked the beginning of my recovery as an adult child and the end of my confusion as a recovering alcoholic. I believe that it was through the fellowship of AA that I learned how to live without booze, and through the fellowship of ACoA (Adult Children of Alcoholics) that I learned to live with myself.

Could I Be A Co-dependent?

I started my journey toward recovery in AA at the age of 24. I was a "high-bottom drunk" — high bottom meaning that I had not lost my liver, my spouse or my job — and the youngest member of my group. Walking into that first AA meeting was a frightening experience. I felt like I was surrounded by people old enough to be my parents. These were *really* old people . . . they were *40*.

Now that I am 40, of course, I have a somewhat different perspective. At the time, I did not really trust anyone over 30. In fact one of my crises in recovery was when I turned 30 and looked into the mirror and said, "I can't trust you anymore."

This was by no means a new revelation. I'd always known intuitively that I didn't really trust myself. I just figured that one day, if I kept working my program, I'd learn to trust in myself again. Besides, I didn't have time for such trivial matters. I was too busy acting the part of "Mr. Recovery" to let a little thing like mistrust get in my way.

Sick as I was, I had managed to get hired as a chemical dependency counselor by one of the local treatment centers. I had been assigned the job of setting up a new outpatient program. I was no longer using chemicals, but I was only three months sober. Talk about the blind leading the blind! My heart was in the right place, but my head was stuck in another orifice.

The treatment center had been doing inpatient care for some time but because of its inherent limitations, prohibitive cost and restrictive flavor, the hospital was under financial pressure to expand its range of services. Outpatient treatment seemed to offer the best potential with the least risk, so off we went. It was a very experimental undertaking and not the kind of project that the tenured professional wanted to gamble on. I had my doubts as well but had nothing to lose.

I may have been crazy, but I was not stupid. I saw the new program as a wonderful opportunity and a chance to carve out a place for myself in the field. It seemed to me like a no-lose situation, and there was no way I was going to let it slip through my fingers. I felt like a kid in a candy store. They gave me a title, an office, a desk, a phone, a swivel chair, a staff and even a raise. The only thing they didn't give me was an instruction manual on how to set up the program.

I knew some basic theory, but outside of a rather spotty professional resume and my rookie status in AA, I had only my personal history to go on. In addition to being an alcoholic, I was also an adult child of an alcoholic — which meant that I had a lot of unconscious empathy and intuitive understanding for both sides of the question. I think it was my own unresolved issues as an adult child that inspired my coming up with the idea of a family-centered treatment program. The hospital management liked the idea, so it was decided that we would invite whole families into the treatment process.

The plan was simple: Take everything we knew about treating the alcoholic and apply it to the rest of the family members. No problem, right? Wrong.

The families came in hordes — children, parents, grandparents, aunts, uncles, cousins, lovers, spouses. Once a week on these family nights we'd get them all together in a group, give them permission to talk and ask if there was anything on their minds or anything they'd like to share about their "alcoholic others." "Would we ever!" they said and out would come the inventories.

Now I don't know what you think a healthy clinical ratio of therapist to patient is, but many were the times that I found myself sitting alone trying to facilitate family groups of 30 or 40 people. I would be totally lost and feel right at home all at the same time. It felt a lot like being back in my own alcoholic family where chaos was the name of the game. So I just sat there, put on one of my best "counselor looks" and took everything in. I listened particularly to the children and the co-dependent adults who spoke not only about their alcoholic marriages but of their own alcoholic families of origin.

As I listened I began to get in touch with my own adult child history and all the stuff that I had never talked about. I had no idea that this was going to happen.

In theory healthy therapists are not supposed to engage in countertransference, displacement of their own issues. But, like so many professionals who had not yet found themselves, I was recovering in part through a process of listening to what I had to say to others and what others had to say to me. It was the voice of the "counselor in the mirror" who spoke to me about my own unfinished issues. I could not run away from it. Every week the same thing would happen until finally it came to me: I was not really a therapist, I was a patient. My next thought was, *"Oh my God, I'm a co-dependent."*

This was a disturbing revelation. Why? Because I was a recovering alcoholic, and the notion of an alcoholic co-dependent was simply unheard of. Traditionally alcoholics and co-dependents had always been thought of as mutually exclusive. You could be one or the other, but not both. The very idea of an alcoholic co-dependent was a serious contradiction in terms.

So, for the first time in an otherwise blissful stroll into sobriety, I was beginning to doubt my own sanity. *"I can't be a co-dependent,"* I told myself, *"I'm not even married to an alcoholic. Oh yeah? Then why do I always feel like a co-dependent when I'm sitting in those groups?"*

I argued back and forth with myself for several days until it finally came to me: It wasn't the spouses of the alcoholics I'd been identifying with, it was their *children.* Their struggles paralleled mine. And it was in the light of their sharing that I first saw myself. I was so excited and relieved to find an answer that I could hardly wait to share my discovery with someone.

Like a typical adult child with something to share, I decided to go and tell my family. In this case it was my AA family. In my naivete I thought they would be really glad to hear what I had to share. I just knew they'd be impressed. No doubt they'd say, "This man is a real genius. We're so lucky that he's a part of our family. Why, if it weren't for him, we'd still be in the dark." So, without giving it another thought, I went directly to my home group to share the good news.

"I am working on my program," I told myself, *"and this is a perfect opportunity to practice some of that 'rigorous honesty' that the old-timers are always touting."* Rigorous honesty, I neglected to remember, can be dangerous in the wrong hands. In a literal sense, it means that you say *everything* that is on your mind.

For example, say you're a newly recovering person with no boundaries and you say to someone you've just met, "Hi! I'm so-and-so and I am an incest victim, my mother is an alcoholic and I'm divorced. I have just been discharged from the hospital and the medications I'm on are helping me deal with my depression." The person who you're talking to goes, "Geez!" and you wonder why they disappear.

Of course I completely dismiss this possibility, go to my AA group and sit down. I'm so excited. I just know that they're really going to want to hear what I have to say. I can hardly wait for my turn to speak. We get through all the opening stuff and one by one we introduce ourselves. When it's my turn I say, "Hi! I'm Bob, a recovering alcoholic and a recovering co-dependent."

There was no turning back now. The co-dependent cat was out of the bag and I was doing my best to act as though I had not said anything out of the ordinary. But on the inside my guts were churning and I was carrying on another one of those private conversations. It was a heated argument that went something like this:

Parent to Child: Boy, it's just like you not to keep your big mouth shut. Why can't you ever leave well enough alone? Why in God's name do you always have to get in there and stir things up?

You never heard anyone else in this group say that they were co-dependent, did you? No, I didn't think so. I suppose the next thing you're going to try and tell them is that they are all co-dependent, too.

You're always trying to change the rules to fit your own selfish interests. Maybe if you spent more time thinking about the needs of others you wouldn't feel so co-dependent. Co-dependency isn't your real problem anyway, just your stinking alcoholic thinking.

Nothing is ever good enough for you, is it? Why don't you face it, Bob. You're just one of the crowd. You're no more co-dependent than the man in the moon. You are just an alcoholic suffering from a chronic case of 'terminal uniqueness,' and that is the way I see it. End of discussion.

Child to Parent: *(No verbal response, only a defiant silence.)*

Adult to Child: *(Picking up where the parent left off:)*

I agree. You are just making a mountain out of a molehill as usual. You've taken this whole co-dependency thing and blown it way out of proportion. Sure, you had some tough times along the way. But that does not mean that you are a co-dependent. Besides, you've had enough training and experience in AA to know that it is not the alcoholic who is the co-dependent.

You see, Bob, what you're saying simply does not make logical sense. You may feel like a co-dependent, but you're not. I just think that somewhere along the road you lost touch with your professional objectivity. You are confusing your

issues with those of your patients. Perhaps it's
time for you to step away from your job and let
someone who is more objective take over.

Why, if I didn't know better, I would say you
were on a dry drunk. Yeah, that's it: You're experiencing a dry drunk! Phew! For a moment there
I was beginning to wonder if you had lost your
mind or something. Now admit it. Underneath it
all, you have been thinking about drinking,
haven't you?

Child to Adult: No, I have *not* been thinking about drinking. At
least not until you brought it up. And I'm not on
a dry drunk either. I'm just trying to tell you how
I feel, but no one seems to want to hear what I
have to say.

It feels just like when I was living at home with
Mom and Dad. They never wanted to listen to me
either. All I want is for you to listen to me the way
you listen to all those other people in treatment.

Oh, what's the use. You care more about them
than you do about me anyway. I hate being me.
Sometimes I wish I had never been born. If I
could be someone else, I would be.

Suddenly I noticed that everyone was staring at me. The introductions had stopped and I knew immediately that I had said something
wrong. My heart started to race and the room temperature felt like
it had just gone up 25 degrees. Things were definitely not going the
way I had imagined.

Who Invited You Anyway?

Finally someone broke the silence. It was a familiar voice, the
oldest guy in our group. He turned toward me, gave me a fatherly
look and said, "Son, this is an Alcoholics Anonymous meeting. If
you think that you have a problem with co-de-pen-den-cy, then
perhaps . . . "

Now the kid in me was following this conversation like a dog on a
hunt. And before he got to the end of his sentence, I heard my inner
child say, *"He's going to send us to Al-Anon."* And sure enough, out of
his mouth came, " . . . you might want to consider going to Al-Anon."

God had spoken. Clearly no one was going to challenge his authority. The message was loud and clear: "We do not want any co-dependents around here."

I heard my anger alarm sound and I heard the child in me say, *"Let me at him, I'll rip the SOB's face off!"* In the past I might have done exactly that, but with two years of sobriety I had managed to achieve at least some semblance of emotional recovery. For the first time ever, I felt my inner adult intervene and pull my inner child out of harm's way. My typical response would have been to turn my back on the child and simply allow him to run rampant. He would have climbed into his Mack truck, slammed it into high gear and dropped the old man in his tracks. Then, just to make sure, he would have checked the rear-view mirror to see if the guy was still twitching. If he was, the child would have put his truck in reverse and hit him again.

Of course the emotional rent for this behavior was always the same: dripping guilt and shame, or what today I choose to refer to as *"shilt."* I think it was my desire to avoid the feeling of shilt that caused the adult in me to step forward in the first place. Whatever the reason, I felt in those few moments that I had turned an important corner in my life.

A sense of calm came over me and I heard my inner adult say to my child, *"No, Bob, we are not going to rip his face off. In fact we are going to do as he says and go to Al-Anon."*

My child shook his head and said, *"Say what? I am not going to Al-Anon. The only people who go to Al-Anon are women. Yuck!"*

It was not that my child did not want to be with women, he did. It was just that he did not trust me to be myself around women. I could hardly blame him — it was not as though we had ever had a healthy long-term relationship with anyone, man or woman. Anyway, my adult says to my child, *"I understand that you do not want to go to Al-Anon but we are going. Besides, you're not in charge here. I am."*

It felt both good and bad to have someone there for me inside: good because my child no longer had to face things alone; bad because it meant he was no longer in control. But nothing changes until something changes, and the adult in me finally realized that it was not the child's responsibility to lead the way.

Co-dependents and adult children have problems with change because they expect their inner child to be in charge — I certainly expected mine to be. And so the idea that he would no longer be leading the way was not something he was willing to accept. As far as he was concerned, there was no one else better qualified. I could tell from the war going on inside my head that my child was not about to give up his position without a fight.

It was a classic battle:

Child: I don't care what you say. I am not going to Al-Anon. You're just like everybody else in my life — you never listen to me. Why should I do what you say anyhow? You've never been there for me before.

Adult: You're right, I haven't been there for you and I'm just beginning to see that now. I want you to know that I feel guilty about that and I am sorry.

Child: Yeah, sure you are.

Adult: I know that you're angry with me and I don't blame you. I would be angry too. Nevertheless I am sorry for abandoning you. Maybe in time you will forgive me.

Child: Excuse me if I don't hold my breath. I've said it before and I'll say it again: Al-Anon is for old ladies and wimps and I am not going!

Adult: Say whatever you like, but the fact remains that we *are* going.

Child: No I'm not!

Adult: Yes you are and, like I said before, it's not your decision anyway. You are no longer driving this bus. *I* am. End of discussion!

Though I didn't know it at the time, I had taken the first important step toward emancipating myself from the grip of co-dependency. Instead of *reacting* to the conflict, I had *responded* to it. And instead of abandoning myself, which would have been the co-dependent thing to do, I had stood up for myself, which was the healing thing to do. I had unconsciously stumbled across a hidden side of my personality that was both mature enough and courageous enough to lead the child in me through the emotional perils of adult life.

Where was my inner parent? I guess he was off in a pew somewhere, praying. No doubt he thought he was doing me some kind of favor, but the last thing I needed at that point were his prayers. A hug maybe, or even an arm around the shoulder would have been nice. But prayers? Give me a break!

Inner parent or no, I was determined to follow through with my plans. So, immediately after leaving — or should I say escaping —

the AA meeting I headed straight for the nearest phone and called the local intergroup office to get a listing of all the Al-Anon meetings in my area.

A couple of days later I found myself sitting smack dab in the middle of my first Al-Anon group. Just as I had expected, it was all women. I heard the kid in me laugh and say, *"I was right, I was right, I told you so, I told you so."* Of course, as he had also predicted, they were all old enough to be my mother.

From the moment I stepped into the room I could feel it happening: They were all looking at me and thinking to themselves, "Our son, he's come home." It was not a pretty sight, but I had come too far to turn back now.

After a few brief announcements the meeting was called to order. The introductions began and when it was my turn, I took a deep breath and blurted out, "Hello, my name is Bob, and I'm a recovering alcoholic and a recovering co-dependent."

Deja vu. The entire group went silent on me. It was like watching an instant replay of a bad dream, only this time I was ready. I had learned from my earlier experience in AA and was prepared for a somewhat less than enthusiastic reception. No one said a word. Finally the oldest woman in the group — the squad leader — looked at me and said, "Son, this is an Al-Anon meeting, and if you think that you're an al-co-hol-ic . . . and Lord knows how we l-o-v-e the al-co-hol-ic, then perhaps . . ."

She didn't have to finish. I knew exactly what she was going to say, and the little kid in me spoke right up: *"She's going to send us back to AA."* *"Right again,"* said my adult. And out of her mouth came the words, " . . . you'd better go to Alcoholics Anonymous."

Hindsight being what it is, I realize now that I had set this whole thing up. AA and Al-Anon had become the unwitting victims of my little drama. Unconsciously I was using them to work out some of my own unfinished business. Collectively they had become a representation of all those authority figures from whom I had yet to emancipate myself, and whose voices were saying to me, *"You do not belong. You are not good enough. You do not do it right. You are a bad person. There's no room for someone like you in our family."*

My past was finally catching up with me. Today I know that we are all destined to continue reenacting to the unresolved issues of our childhood. Most adult children/co-dependents have never really left home. This is why most can never have a healthy marriage. They get married to the people who live inside them, and those people are often nothing more than a memory of their parents. They marry their mother and father and end up doing the very things they said they would never do. It is a crazy paradox to think that the very people we are trying to get close to are also the very people we are trying to get away from. There's a song by Michael Brown entitled *I Have Got a Tendency Towards Co-dependency* that sums it up nicely in one line: "I *love* you, *hate* you, *want* you, so *leave me alone*."

I managed to sit through the balance of the meeting without getting into it with the old lady. But inside, the usual amount of self-talk was going on:

Child: I knew it. I knew it. They don't want us either. Now what?

Adult: Don't worry, I've got everything in hand.

Child: Oh, yeah, since when?

Adult: Relax, kid, I know what I'm doing.

Child: And just what is it that you're going to do?

Adult: Well, one thing's for sure. We are going to go back to AA.

Child: Go back? What are you, nuts? I don't think you understand. They don't want us to come back.

Adult: Perhaps not, but we are going back just the same.

Child: Oh, great. You want to go back and get our butts kicked some more.

Adult: We are not going to get our butts kicked.

Child: You must be a glutton for punishment. They already told us that they do not cater to people like us.

Adult: I heard what they said, but they don't have the right to keep us from going back.

Child: I wouldn't be too sure about that if I were you.

Adult: Well, like the program says, we are just going to have to let go and let God.

Child: That's it? That's your plan?

Adult: No, actually there is something more that we are going to do.

Child: Like what?

Adult: First, we are going to go to the library and do a little investigative research on AA.

Child: Investigative research? What's that?

Adult: Never mind, all you have to do is sit back and leave the driving to me.

Then, out of nowhere, I heard the parent in me praying, *"Lord, help us!"*

Just Another Day
In Court

Every adult child co-dependent is a lawyer at heart. It is the co-*defendant* in them who is always expecting the worst. For example, whenever they are in *inter*personal conflict (with one or more other people) they go into a mock rehearsal with themselves in an effort to try and control the outcome: *"When I see that person, I'm going to say this and then they're going to say that, then I'll come back with this and they'll come back at me with that, and then I'll jump over here and they'll jump over there, then I'll hit them with this and they'll try to hit me with that, and in the end I'll be on top and they'll be on the bottom."*

I was especially good at this co-defendant game whenever I felt that I had been righteously wronged — which was exactly how I felt in this particular case. Every part of me — my inner parent, my inner adult and my inner child — believed that we had been poorly treated by our 12-Step family and deserved another chance to be heard. Being the flaming co-dependent co-defendant that I was, I went hog wild and poured everything I had into preparing myself for my day in court.

For two weeks I ran around like a crazy man, searching out every bit of information on AA and Al-Anon that I could get my hands on. I was looking for something that would lend credence to my position. I fancied myself a real Clarence Darrow, champion of justice and defender of the faith. What I would become, in fact, was a missionary zealot who couldn't see the forest for the trees. In other words, a real pain in the butt.

On the positive side I did manage to learn a fair amount about AA and its co-founders, Dr. Bob and Bill W. During my research I came upon a letter written by Bill W. in which he spoke of something he referred to as "emotional recovery," a stage in sobriety that went far beyond mere abstinence from alcohol. This dimension called for absolute surrender of all outside dependencies — an issue that sounded to me like co-dependency.

Unfortunately Bill W. had died ten years earlier and was unavailable for comment. So I took it upon myself to make my own conclusions. I knew it was a questionable call, but I was in desperate need of finding some credible resource from which to draw. And who was more credible than Bill W., the father of AA? Armed with this new information, I was ready to try it again.

Back Again

I gathered up my notes and headed back to AA with my findings. I arrived just in time for the introductions, sat myself down, and blurted out, "Hello, I'm Bob, an alcoholic and co-dependent."

Once again a deafening silence fell over the group. It was as if I had never left. Everyone was holding onto their seats. I had thrown out the bait and as expected, the old man took it hook, line and sinker. He turned to me and said in a clearly condescending tone of voice, "Son, do we have to go through this whole thing again?"

This time the adult in me seized the moment and replied firmly, "Yes, sir, I believe we do. But first I'd like to ask you a couple of basic questions. Do you mind?"

"Fire away," the old man said.

The thought crossed my child's mind to do just that — fire away. But once again the adult in me stepped in and took over. I could actually feel the adult stop my child from going off the deep end. Somehow, in the midst of battle, I had found the courage to stand up for myself and be the kind of adult I had always wanted to be. My child still had his doubts about the new adult—once burned, twice shy. But the appearance of this big person inside me was an improvement over the earlier model, who could only be counted on not to be counted on.

As I sat there watching the drama unfold I realized that I was no longer a helpless victim. I could choose to stand up for myself. For the first time I recognized that I had been a victim as a child; that I had been emotionally abandoned by my parents, who were sick; and that none of it had been my fault. I was innocent by virtue of the fact that I had no choice in the matter. But now as an adult I had a choice. It was no longer my parents' fault, nor the fault of my inner child. It was my failure as a parent and adult to myself that was at the core of my self-abandonment. Without realizing it I had graduated from childhood victim to adult volunteer.

This was a difficult pill for me to swallow because it meant that I could no longer use my mother or father as a scapegoat for every mistake, failed relationship or missed opportunity in my life. True enough, they helped to set the stage for what I learned to do later, which was abandon myself. But beyond that they were not to blame. Somehow, through my memories, they had managed to take up residence in my head. As I grew older these memories would become the blueprints for the creation of my own inner parent and adult.

It seems ironic to think that our inner child's negative memories of Mom and Dad are destined, if left unresolved, to become the materials out of which we will construct a model of our own inner adult and parent. Who would have thought that the very people we thought we were leaving behind would be the very people we would end up inviting back into our lives? And not just as models for our inner parent and adult, but as prototypes for the kinds of people we would eventually marry, work for, be friends with and even vote for.

What a slap in the face this realization was to me! Like so many of my early awakenings in recovery it was bittersweet. It was bitter in the sense that I felt angry, hurt, guilty and ashamed over what I had done to myself. But it was sweet because I was excited, relieved and overjoyed to think that my days of co-dependency, self-abuse, denial and abandonment were finally coming to an end. The clouds of confusion that had always surrounded my life in AA were starting to clear. And as I would come to discover, it was not my child who stood in the way of my emotional recovery, it was my inner parent and adult. For the moment it seemed enough just to know that I was not alone within myself and that we seemed to be headed in the right direction.

Co-dependency is what I would call a proactive dis-ease of the spirit. This dis-ease is all about the unfinished business of our past getting in the way of what is going on in our present. An adult child/co-dependent always gets yesterday mixed up with today, so that whenever something happens in the here-and-now, it triggers off some unresolved feelings from the past. We are pulled back in time and react to the current situation as though it were yesterday's event. The adult child/co-dependent retreats into whatever form of behavior he or she used in the past to get through. It's not a pretty picture, but it's precisely what happens whenever we abandon ourselves and leave the child in our spirit in charge.

My Adult Takes Charge

Meanwhile back at the AA meeting, things were really beginning to heat up. The child in me was sitting on the edge of his chair, his gun cocked. My parent was off in the rear of the room, still praying. And my adult was just starting his cross-examination of the old man — Mr. AA:

Adult: To start with I'd like to know if you can be kicked out of Alcoholics Anonymous.

Mr. AA: Of course not. What an absurd question to ask.

Adult: Maybe, but I get the distinct feeling that I could be the first.

Mr. AA: Don't you think you're over-reacting just a tad?

Adult: No, on the contrary. I think it's you and the rest of this group who are over-reacting.

Mr. AA: Oh, really? And how is that?

Adult: Well, to begin with, you are acting like being an alcoholic and a co-dependent is some kind of violation of AA tradition.

Mr. AA: Well, I believe it is.

Adult: No, not according to everything that I have read—and I have read just about everything ever published on the subject. In fact, according to chapter five of the Big Book of AA, there is only one requirement for membership in the program, and that is a desire to stop drinking. Is that right?

Mr. AA: Of course that's right, but what in God's name does it have to do with anything?

Adult: Everything, as far as I'm concerned. The whole conflict here seems to be about whether or not it is okay for me to be who I think I am and still be part of AA.

Mr. AA: Excuse me, Bob, I don't mean to interrupt your train of thought, but I was wondering if you had gone to Al-Anon as I suggested.

Adult: Yes, as a matter of fact I did go to Al-Anon. And you know what? They sent me back here. It seems they feel the same about alcoholics going to Al-Anon as you do about co-dependents going to AA.

Mr. AA: I think you're taking this whole thing out of context, Bob.

Adult: Wrong again. I'm simply trying to get it back into perspective. Take chapter five of the Big Book, for example, where it says, 'If you have decided you want what we have and are willing to go to *any length* to get it — then you're *willing* to take certain steps.' — *Any length* being the operative words here — 'With all the earnestness at our command, we beg you to be *fearless* and *thorough* from the very start' — *fearless* — and *thorough* is exactly what I'm being — *'Half measures* availed us nothing' — *half measures,* in this case, meaning that I would continue to deny who I am.*

Mr. AA: I know perfectly well what it says in the book, but I'd still like to know what that has to do with the question at hand.

Adult: (At that point I stopped talking, reached into my pocket, pulled out my two-year sobriety medallion and read the inscription that was written around the outside edge.) *To Thine Own Self Be True.* That's the question here. How will we ever recover if we refuse to be true to ourselves?

Mr. AA: Very dramatic, Bob. But I still don't see what that has to do with the mission of AA, which is to get sober. My concern, Bob, is that this need of yours to be something other than just an alcoholic — which is all that I think you are — is going to poison your sobriety.

Adult: I have heard you use that line before as an excuse not to let others in the group look honestly at the emotional side

---

* *Sources for quotes used in this book will be found in the notes section beginning on page 203.*

of their sobriety, and quite frankly I'm not buying it. I do not believe that Bill W. was poisoning his sobriety when he started to talk about his co-dependency — or, in his words, 'faulty emotional dependencies.' Moreover he felt strongly enough about the whole issue and its relationship to the quality of one's sobriety that he decided to write about it in a letter to a fellow alcoholic whose sobriety Bill saw being threatened by these faulty emotional dependencies.

I just happen to have a copy of that letter. If you would not mind too terribly, I'd like to share it with the group.

Mr. AA: By all means. I'm sure we would all love to hear what Bill W. had to say on the subject. That way we can all make up our minds as to what we think.

Adult: My thought exactly. And if anyone is at all interested as to where I found this letter, I got it from the January 1958 issue of the AA *Grapevine*. The title of the letter as it appeared in that issue was, 'Emotional Recovery.'

This is the letter I read to the group:

Emotional Recovery

I think that many oldsters who have put our AA "booze cure" to severe but successful tests still find they often lack emotional sobriety. Perhaps they will be the spearhead for the next major development in AA, the development of much more real maturity and balance (which is to say, humility) in our relations with ourselves, with our fellows and with God.

Those adolescent urges that so many of us have for top approval, perfect security and perfect romance, urges quite appropriate to age 17, proved to be an impossible way of life when we are at age 47 and 57.

Since AA began, I have taken immense wallops in all these areas because of my failure to grow up emotionally and spiritually. My God, how painful it is to keep demanding the impossible and how very painful to discover, finally, that all along we have had the cart before the horse. Then comes the final agony of seeing how awfully wrong we have been, but still finding ourselves unable to get off the emotional merry-go-round.

How to translate a right mental conviction into a right emotional result, and so into easy, happy and good living? Well, that is not only the neurotic's problem, it is the problem of life itself for all of us who have got to the point of real willingness to hew to right principles in all our affairs.

Even then, as we hew away, peace and joy may still elude us. That is the place so many of us AA oldsters have come to. And it is a hell of a spot, literally. How shall our unconscious, from which so many of our fears, compulsions, phoney aspirations still stream, be brought into line with what we actually believe, know and want! How to convince our dumb, raging and hidden "Mr. Hyde" becomes our main task.

I have recently come to believe that this can be achieved. I believe so because I begin to see many benighted ones, folks like you and me, commencing to get results. Last autumn, depression, having no really rational cause at all, took me to the cleaners. I began to be scared that I was in for another long chronic spell. Considering the grief I have had with depressions, it was not a bright prospect.

I kept asking myself, "Why can't the 12 Steps work to release depression?" By the hour, I stared at the St. Francis Prayer . . ."It is better to comfort than to be comforted." Here was the formula, all right, but why didn't it work?

Suddenly, I realized what the matter was. My basic flaw had always been dependence, almost absolute dependence, on people or circumstances to supply me with prestige, security and the like. Failing to get these things according to my perfectionist dreams and specifications, I had fought for them. And when defeat came, so did my depression.

There was not a chance of making the outgoing love of St. Francis a workable and joyous way of life until these fatal and almost absolute dependencies were cut away.

Because I had over the years undergone a little spiritual development, the absolute quality of these frightful dependencies had never before been so starkly revealed. Reinforced by what grace I could secure in prayer, I found I had to exert every ounce of will and action to cut off these faulty emotional dependencies upon people, upon AA, indeed, upon any act of circumstance whatsoever.

Then only could I be free to love as Francis did. Emotional and instinctual satisfactions, I saw, were really the extra dividends of having love, offering love and expressing love appropriate to each relation of life. Plainly, I could not avail myself to God's love until I was able to offer it back to Him by loving others as He would have me. I could not possibly do that so long as I was victimized by false dependencies.

For me dependence meant demand, a demand for the possession and control of the people and the conditions surrounding me.

While those words "absolute dependence" may look like a gimmick, they were the ones that helped to trigger my release into my present degree of stability and quietness of mind, qualities which I am now trying to consolidate by offering love to others regardless of the return to me.

This seems to be the primary healing circuit, an outgoing love of God's creation and His people, by means of which we avail ourselves of His love for us. It is most clear that the real current cannot flow until our paralyzing dependencies are broken, and broken at depth. Only then can we possibly have a glimmer of what adult love really is.

If we examine every disturbance we have, great or small, we will find at the root of it some unhealthy dependence and its consequent demand. Let us, with God's help, continually surrender these hobbling demands. Then we can be set free to live and love. We may then be able to gain emotional sobriety.

Of course, I haven't offered you a really new idea . . . only a gimmick that has started to unhook several of my own "hexes" at depth. Nowadays my brain no longer races compulsively in either elation, grandiosity or depression. "I have been given a quiet place in bright sunshine."

—Bill W.

I paused a moment and continued with my ideas.

Adult: As far as I'm concerned, what Bill W. is talking about in his letter is what I am calling my co-dependency. And, like Bill, I am trying to recover from my co-dependency and recover my emotional life.

Mr. AA: Fine. You're trying to recover your emotional life. Good for you. So, are you finished?

Adult: No, as a matter of fact I'm not. There are just a couple more things that I would like to say.

First of all, I have figured out that you are not in charge here and that I have a right to my opinion whether you like it or not.

Second, I do not need your permission to be a member of this group.

Third, I plan on continuing to be a part of this group for as long as I am sucking air!

And last but not least, I want you to know that if you do not like the way things are going, then you can go out and find yourself another group. Because I like it here, and as I said before, I am not leaving.

Overcoming Resistance

No one spoke another word, and the meeting went on as though nothing had happened. After a few meetings, however, others in the group began to look at themselves and question whether or not they were really working their program or just playing it safe. All systems resist change. The old ideas were being challenged and like all families that feel threatened, it was inevitable that there would be some resistance.

In principle, resistance is not a bad thing. It serves as a kind of internal governor that helps to preserve the connecting tissue of the family. It is a positive force that protects the system from over-reacting to change or breaking apart. It is not healthy resistance that is harmful to the system; the real threat is unhealthy resistance, which allows for no change or growth to take place. AA is a family. As such it needs to remain open to change, while at the same time protecting and preserving the integrity and clarity of its purpose: to help alcoholic/chemically dependent/co-dependent people to stop medicating themselves and recover their emotional lives.

As a loving critic and loyal member of AA and Al-Anon I have come to appreciate the lessons of "Keep it simple," "First things first" and "One day at a time." I have also come to appreciate that in order to recover our emotional lives, we need to move beyond mere abstinence and detachment from our primary drug of choice (be it booze, sex, food, work, relationships or religion) and let go completely of all our faulty emotional dependencies as well. Yes, we need to make abstinence and detachment our first objective. But once this has been accomplished, we need to set our sights on the long-range goal: recovering our family within.

Recovering the family within requires more than just our application of the 12 Steps to a program of maintenance. It requires us to integrate practice, and apply these principles in all our affairs — not only as they relate to our interactions with others, but as they relate to our interactions with ourselves. The 12 Steps are not a set of rigid rules, they are a suggested program for living that emphasizes progress, not perfection. Moreover, it is not the 12 Steps that stand in the way of our progress toward recovering the family within, it is the people who misinterpret the steps who do that. Like the child in your spirit, the 12 Steps are perfect. It is a dysfunctional parent and adult who, in the spirit of these two families, AA and Al-Anon, keep us divided from ourselves.

Until those agents of change — our inner adult and parent — truly let go and break free of the dysfunctional rules of their past, the chances of real growth and lasting change are slim to none.

PART TWO

My Family,
My Self

So where did things go wrong?

I believe the answer to this question lies within the workings of the family system. Genetics aside, we are all the product of the systems from which we came. This is an age-old notion and one that has given rise to what is now called *family systems theory.*

For some time now many systems theorists, such as Virginia Satir, Murray Bowen and Salvador Minuchin have been saying that in order for us to truly understand ourselves, we must first come to a basic understanding of those systems from which we came. These systems include our nuclear family (parents and siblings), our extended family (grandparents, in-laws and other blood relatives or relatives by adoption) and our sociocultural family (race, religion and nationality).

Over the past 15 years I have come to recognize and appreciate, personally and professionally, the powerful role these systems play in shaping our lives. More important, however, my experience has taught me that in order to break free of the past, I must first be willing to face it. This is an unavoidable truth about the process of change and one that brings us face to face with ourselves. Real success in life depends on our willingness to be ourselves while embracing the whole of our experience.

I have heard it said that there is no such thing as revolution, only evolution. From this perspective everything we think, feel or do could be viewed as a part of a metaphorical expression of where we have been. For example, my feelings of mistrust as an adult are nothing more than a picture of my mistrust as a child. In any case, the experience of life is meant to be a process of becoming, not an exercise in survival.

Unfortunately many of us came from war-torn families. They taught us to fear the process of life through the experience of abandonment, rejection, neglect and abuse. As children of these troubled families we learned to survive, but we failed to develop emotionally. The end result was that we were destined to become a part of yet another adult child/co-dependent generation.

For us the process of development was turned inside out. Instead of learning to face the intrapersonal (within ourselves) conflicts of life, we learned to avoid the truth by becoming overly involved with and manipulative of outside activities. In the beginning these patterns of coping simply represented a creative effort to avoid pain and punishment. But the underlying foundations of our avoidance behavior remained with us; and what had once been the innocent maneuvers of a troubled child ended up becoming the dysfunctional maneuvers of a co-dependent adult.

According to developmental theorists, such as Erik Erikson and Jean Piaget, we humans must go through specific stages on the road to becoming a whole person. A child who is unsuccessful at working through the various stages of identity formation will inevitably experience delay in the developmental process.

The concept of identity development has been around for some time, but we have only recently come to appreciate the fundamental role that it plays in intimacy and co-dependency. Confusing as it may seem, identity and co-dependency are opposite ends of the same developmental continuum: Intimacy and clear identity at one end, and co-dependency or unclear identity at the other.

Despite the obvious disparity that exists between these two extremes, both are rooted in the same developmental soil. In fact the stages of identity development are flexible and subject to modification. Consequently, if we choose to, we can change the course of our own identity by confronting the past and challenging the co-dependent rules that keep us from knowing who we really are.

In short, we have the power to overcome our history and redefine our identity.

The Co-dependent
Dimension

What follows is a short course on the basics of co-dependency. If you believe that you are already well grounded in the subject, then feel free to jump ahead. If you are a newcomer to the subject, please take some time to go through this chapter before you move on to the next.

I say "take some time" for a good reason. If you are like the majority of adult children, you are probably having some difficulty with what psychologists call *postponement of gratification* — like a dog with a bone, a child with a candy bar or an alcoholic with a drink. For most adult child/co-dependents patience is not a well-understood virtue. We want what we want and we want it *now* — who cares about the consequences? Consequently we tend to find ourselves in difficult situations where we end up feeling tricked, blindsided, victimized, embarrassed, ashamed, remorseful and up the proverbial creek without a paddle.

We scold ourselves: "How could I have been so stupid? Why do I always seem to get myself into this position? I just didn't think. Won't I ever learn?"

We hurt ourselves and others because we are unable to postpone gratification. We say that we are sorry, but after a while, just saying we are sorry is not enough.

It has taken me the better part of the last ten years to begin to understand in depth the meaning of co-dependency and its relationship to my life struggles. So please be patient when you read through this chapter. Give yourself as much time as you need to absorb the information.

Before we begin I'd like to add one more bit of sage advice: The majority of mistakes I have made in my life were not due to a lack of intelligence but to a lack of information. By the same token, co-dependency is not due to a lack of intelligence. As I tell my clients who see their co-dependency as a reflection of their lack of gray matter, you're not stupid. It takes a lot of brains to get yourself this screwed up! Think about that for a moment.

In over 15 years of treatment experience, I have never met a mentally retarded co-dependent. The reason for this is simple: Mentally retarded people aren't trying to con anyone into believing that they are someone they're not. They do not hide their feelings. If they are experiencing something emotionally, they let you know. If they are sad, they cry — they do not get angry. When they are mad, they act mad — they do not mask it. When they feel happy, they show it. When they want to hug, they hug. When they give, they give unconditionally.

Oh yes, there is one more thought I would like to share with you — especially if you see yourself as hopelessly stuck. The good news is, you're not stuck. The bad news is you *are* getting worse. My personal and professional experiences have taught me that life never stands still and that co-dependency is a dis-ease over which we have a choice.

"Recovery is not a matter of chance, but a matter of *choice*." You have a right to your beliefs, but not if they are unhealthy. These thoughts will only serve to keep you from taking hold of your life.

The Basics Of Co-dependency

First, co-dependency exists. It is a definable, primary, progressive and chronic dis-ease that if left untreated, will lead to the premature death of the body, mind or spirit. And death, in any of these three respects, is about as chronic as life gets. Figure 4-1 shows the progression of co-dependency.

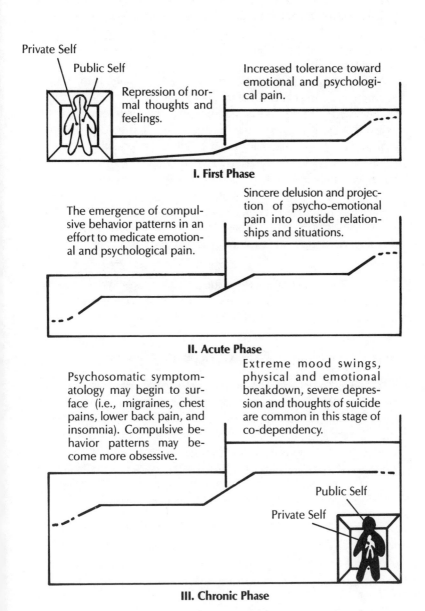

Private Self

Public Self

Repression of normal thoughts and feelings.

Increased tolerance toward emotional and psychological pain.

I. First Phase

The emergence of compulsive behavior patterns in an effort to medicate emotional and psychological pain.

Sincere delusion and projection of psycho-emotional pain into outside relationships and situations.

II. Acute Phase

Psychosomatic symptomatology may begin to surface (i.e., migraines, chest pains, lower back pain, and insomnia). Compulsive behavior patterns may become more obsessive.

Extreme mood swings, physical and emotional breakdown, severe depression and thoughts of suicide are common in this stage of co-dependency.

Public Self

Private Self

III. Chronic Phase

Figure 4.1. The Progression Of Co-dependency Within The Spirit

Second, co-dependency affects only adults. It is not a childhood dis-ease. Developmentally, children do not possess complete freedom of choice. They are therefore victims whose apparent co-dependent behaviors are only reflections of the unhealthy environment in which they live.

This is not to say that children do not need or require help. They do. But only an adult as defined by age and intellectual capability can be diagnosed as co-dependent. It is the ability to exercise freedom of choice that distinguishes adults from children and co-dependents from victims. Adults may have been childhood victims themselves, but they can no longer be viewed as innocent bystanders in the discussion of co-dependency. They are now the adult volunteers.

To have been ignorant of one's choices is an understandable explanation, but it is by no means a legitimate excuse for failure to act on one's own behalf. Perhaps the only reasonable defense to offer a co-dependent adult volunteer is that to err is human.

You Have Free Choice: The voluntary surrender of free choice as an adult marks an individual's passage into co-dependency.

The Rules Of The Co-dependent System

The term co-dependent was first used to describe the person whose life had been adversely affected as a result of living with someone who was alcoholic or chemically dependent. In those early days the spouse, lover, friend or child of the chemically dependent person was viewed as *co*-dependent. More recently, however, professionals have come to recognize that co-dependency is a family dis-ease — the product of a sick system where certain destructive overt (spoken) or covert (unspoken) rules exist. These rules . . .

- Interfere with the normal process of psycho-emotional development
- Close off and discourage healthy communication
- Ultimately hinder or destroy a system's ability to grow and develop
- Foster mistrust
- Divide the system from within
- Make both interpersonal and intrapersonal intimacy impossible.

Where the rules of co-dependency thrive, intimacy dies.

We learn how to live our lives and interact with others as we grow up. The rules that guide us are passed down from one generation to the next — not by heredity or genetics, but by listening, watching and mimicking. The longer we practice living by the rules of our history, the greater the chances are they will become a permanent part of our future. They will guide the way we manage our relationships with others and with ourselves.

If the rules we practice are dysfunctional, the relationships we develop also will be dysfunctional. Just as water seeks its own level, the rules we practice compel us to pair with others who live by a similar set of rules.

Now it doesn't require a great deal of time or energy to sort out the dysfunctional rules of a co-dependent system. Why? Because the majority of rules specific to co-dependency begin with two familiar words: *Do not* . . .

- *Do not* talk about your problems.
- *Do not* talk about your feelings.
- *Do not* think or feel anything.
- *Do not* trust.

These first four rules are the main pillars of co-dependency and the primary roadblocks to identity development. But there are more.

- *Do not* make mistakes.
- *Do not* ask questions.
- *Do not* be needy.
- *Do not* be selfish.
- *Do not* be yourself.
- *Do not* rock the boat.
- *Do not* have fun.
- *Do not* talk about sex.
- *Do not* get too close or too intimate.

Intimacy and sex are mutually exclusive, but under some circumstances they may go hand in hand. Most adult child/co-dependents have had the unsatisfying and sad experience of sex without intimacy. Finally, the most chilling rule of co-dependency:

- *Do not* be.

Just don't be. This is the chilling bottom line of co-dependency.

These dysfunctional rules effectively block the path of our journey toward self. Instead of developing a clear identity, the individual living under the influence of these dysfunctional rules develops a chameleon-like identity. We learn to conform to outside pressures in order to blend in, and we disguise our true self. Eventually this insidious style of coping leads to an unconscious emotional and psychological division within the spirit that separates us from ourselves and from others.

The dysfunctional rules of a co-dependent system give rise to a self-protective identity that outwardly changes but inwardly remains unchanged. Once these rules have been passed on, they become a dysfunctional and debilitating part of our inner life. The same rules that at one time served the common good and collective purpose of survival in the family now diminish the common good and obstruct our search for a clear and functional identity.

To escape the negative fallout of our collective histories *we must risk change.* We need to take the lessons of the past and endeavor to expand on them. Paradoxically, the legacy of survivorship can serve as a solid foundation on which to build a clear and lasting relationship with ourselves. We have, in the first world at least, been delivered into a time where the quest for self-actualization is no longer a senseless waste of valuable time.

For those of us who have been afforded the opportunities of this New Age, the pursuit of self-actualization is more than just a luxury. It is a responsibility.

If we think of our global family as a single being, then we might begin to conceive of how the dis-ease of co-dependency could have literally entered into the collective spirit of humankind and interfered with its innate drive to evolve and grow. You and I, our nuclear and extended families, and our society as a whole are all systems that need to grow and mature if we are to survive.

In the truest sense, co-dependency is a systems dis-ease that is firmly rooted in the soil of the sociocultural, nuclear, extended and intrapersonal families. It is a *proactive* dis-ease that is transmitted across the generations through a blind adherence to the dysfunctional rules of the past. The learnings, beliefs and rules of the past continue to interfere with the experiences of the present. And it is a proactive dis-ease of the interpersonal system where the losses, hurts and wounds of the past continue to drive a psycho-emotional wedge between the members of the intrapersonal family as well.

The Common Traits Of Co-dependency

Co-dependents have a number of traits in common:

1. **Difficulty identifying feelings accurately**: "Am I angry, lonely, sad or scared?"
2. **Difficulty expressing feelings**: "If I were a woman, it might be all right to cry." "If I were a man, it would be all right for me to be angry."
3. **Difficulty adjusting to change**: "If I take that new job, I'll have to make all new friends." "I don't understand why things can't stay the same between us."
4. **Difficulty making decisions**: "I can't decide because I don't want to make any mistakes. If I do it wrong, they'll never give me another chance."
5. **Difficulty letting go**: "If I don't take care of it, no one will." "I can't leave you because you wouldn't be able to handle it." "I'll never forgive them for what they did to me."
6. **Difficulty dealing with conflict**: "I'm afraid to tell you what I really think because you might leave me." "If I say no, you won't ask me out again."
7. **Difficulty overcoming shame**: "My mistakes are really evidence that I'm no good." "I never graduated from high school so I'm not as good as other people."
8. **Difficulty setting boundaries**: "My children are an extension of me." "I/you have no right to privacy." "I don't know where you end and I begin." "If you don't feel good, then I don't feel good."
9. **Difficulty being flexible**: "There is only one way to do things and that is my way." "Anyone who does not agree with me is wrong." "It was good enough for my parents and it is good enough for me."
10. **Difficulty with people-pleasing**: "Just tell me what you want me to do and I'll do it if it makes you happy." "I will do whatever you want to get you to love me." "I need to get your approval in order to feel good about myself."
11. **Difficulty postponing gratification**: "I want what I want when I want it." "If I think it, I have to say it." "I have to do it right now."
12. **Difficulty forming and maintaining close or intimate relationships**: "I want to be close to you but I've been hurt before and I don't want to get hurt again." "If I let my guard down and get too close, you might not like what

you see." "My parents had a bad marriage and I wouldn't like that to happen to me."

Clearly there is little positive to say about the co-dependent life-style. But buried within the oyster is the pearl of its salvation: Co-dependents are masters of survival. The experience of co-dependency does force one to develop a creative, tenacious, and perse-vering spirit. Paradoxically, then, the very experience that denied life becomes the foundation experience that makes having a life possible.

I believe my experience as a co-dependent taught me survival and gave me the strength to face the truth about my life. Like a phoenix rising from the ashes, the conflicts and rubble of my past were destined to become the foundation of my future.

Coming To Terms With Co-dependency

Let's take another look at the definition of co-dependency: *A delayed identity development syndrome characterized by a psycho-logical, emotional and behavioral pattern of coping that develops as a result of one's prolonged exposure to and practice of a set of dysfunctional family or social rules.*

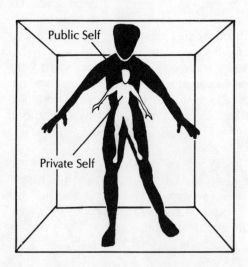

In light of this definition it is reasonable to say that co-dependency is a systems dis-ease that is passed on from one individual to the next through the dysfunctional rules of our social, nuclear and extended families. It is an *inter*personal as well as *intra*personal dis-ease that is defined by the dysfunctional rules of the family.

From a systems perspective, the whole of an individual's co-dependency is greater than the sum of its parts: The co-dependency of a single family member is more than just the reflection of his or her own interpersonal dis-ease; it is also reflective of his or her extended family system. Consequently, co-dependency does not discriminate between systems. *Any system that practices the dysfunctional rules outlined earlier will become co-dependent through and through.*

> *WHAT IS DIS-EASE? I've used the term "dis-ease" quite a bit so far, and you may be wondering just what the heck I mean. Webster's dictionary defines* disease *as "an abnormal condition of an organism or part, especially as a consequence of infection, inherent weakness or environmental stress that impairs the normal physiological functioning."*
>
> *Dis-ease, as it relates to co-dependency, refers to the abnormal division between the intrapersonal spirit as a result of one's adherence to or practice of a set of dysfunctional rules, which impair the normal psycho-emotional functioning of the intrapersonal system.*
>
> *Therefore the state of dis-ease within the spirit can ultimately lead to an actual disease of the physical body.*

The dysfunctional rules of a system — don't talk about the problem, don't feel, don't have fun, don't rock the boat, don't get too close — clearly represent a chronic source of environmental stress that eventually translates into internal stress. The system, be it *inter*personal or *intra*personal, becomes increasingly dependent on the practice of these dysfunctional rules to manage the external psycho-emotional stress of life.

If we assume that an otherwise healthy pattern of coping existed in the first place, then it must be the internalization of these dysfunctional co-dependent rules that ultimately upsets the internal balance of the system and divides the family from itself. So it is that the co-dependent experiences a dis-ease of body, mind and spirit. In a general sense co-dependency is a relationship dis-ease where the adherence to or practice of dysfunctional rules interferes with the "normal" or "healthy" growth and development within the system. Thus we can make a distinction between *early onset* and *late onset* co-dependency.

An early onset co-dependent develops an adult co-dependency as a result of having grown up under a set of dysfunctional family rules. This person, also referred to as an *adult child,* comes from a troubled family background—an alcoholic, chemically dependent, mentally disturbed, physically or sexually abusive or rigidly fundamentalist family.

The late onset co-dependent is *not* an adult child, but one who gets into a troubled relationship or family system as an adult. In the process of trying to adapt, such people end up forsaking the healthier lessons of their past and begin to comply with the dysfunctional rules of that relationship or family they joined as an adult.

Most co-dependents are of the early onset, adult child variety. Generally speaking adult children are always co-dependent, but co-dependents are not always adult children. Although developmentally speaking, late onset and early onset co-dependents are very different, they all suffer from a division of their intrapersonal family.

Despite their varying histories, both types of co-dependents share the same core issues: The rules they follow are dysfunctional, causing the normal growth and development of the intrapersonal family — self-identity — to be stunted.

As children we do not see how the dysfunctional rules that we live by can cause us to be at odds with ourselves. Children experience the negative residual effects of their presence, but they are in no position to pinpoint the source of this emotional fallout. In the absence of a clear understanding or explanation, children end up blaming themselves for whatever conflicts or problems these dysfunctional rules cause in the family.

In my own family of origin I learned early on that there were certain rules of decorum which, if followed, would keep me out of hot water. These rules were not always well defined, however, so I usually learned them through a process of trial and error.

For example, in my family — as in many troubled families — we had a lot of unspoken rules, such as: Do not bring up Mom's drinking or say anything to upset her. Unfortunately, because of the "no talk" communication style in my family, the way I learned that it was not okay to mention Mom's drinking was by mentioning it. I may have been young, but I wasn't stupid. Once I had suffered the consequences of having stuck my foot in my mouth, I never did it again.

The avoidance of pain and punishment through repression and denial is not an unusual reaction for children. In fact it is normal for a child to try and end-run the experience of pain and punishment. As an adult, however, these immature patterns of side-stepping conflict are classic reflections of co-dependency and a delayed identity development.

There are, of course, exceptions to every rule. And under certain conditions — natural disasters, war and being lost in the woods — survival skills are a good thing. So it is not necessarily a bad thing that a system or an individual knows how to survive. But the application of these skills when there is no real threat to one's life are no longer an asset but a liability.

The healthy system knows when it is being victimized, the dysfunctional system does not. *You are never a victim unless someone is pointing a gun to your head or otherwise threatening your life.* The only true victim is one who has *no choice.* To believe otherwise is to deny reality and surrender your personal responsibility.

Changing From
The Inside Out

Our inner spirit has only two real enemies: war and co-dependency. Both conditions are created by people and both carry the extreme, but very real possibility of death. It is not, however, the literal fact of death that is the threat to our spirit, but our *fear* of death.

Our fear of death underlies our fear of change. Change, like death, means crossing over into the unknown. We fear change as we fear death because we are unable to see what lies beyond it. In our family within, it is the child who fears change, equates it with death and believes that what lies beyond is a fate worse than death.

It is precisely this kind of immature logic that fuels an adult's neurotic fear of change. If it were true that change meant death, then none of us would be here today. Now that's an interesting thought!

If we allow our fear of the unknown to control us, we will always be sitting on the sidelines waiting for someone else to make the first move. Co-dependents are classic sideliners in the game of life. They fear change because they believe that they might lose what they have — even though what they have may be nothing at all.

In order to leave this crazy logic behind and let go of all our co-dependent fear of change, we must first be willing to reach out and ask for help. This is no small task. It means coming face to face with the very things we are afraid of: losing control, getting hurt, being rejected or abandoned.

I know how scary this can be because I had to do it myself. It is, however, a necessary leap of faith, and one that we need to make if we are ever to develop a healthy sense of trust in ourselves.

The lack of basic trust is a central theme in the problems of an adult child/co-dependent's life and lies at the core of their sick logic. As I see it, the fear of change in life is directly proportionate to the lack of trust. More than a lack of trust in others, our fear of change is due to a lack of trust in ourselves.

The Developmental Stages

In terms of personal development, learning to trust is the first lesson in everyone's life. In fact many professionals believe that the individual who does not develop basic trust in self and others during infancy will continue to operate without trust as an adult.

According to Erik Erikson's work on human development, we go through eight primary stages of psycho-emotional growth during the course of our lives.* For our purposes we will focus on only the first six stages of this developmental model (see Figure 5-1).

1. Trust *versus* Mistrust (6 months to 18 months)
2. Autonomy *versus* Shame and Doubt (1 to 1½ years)
3. Initiative *versus* Guilt (2 to 6 years)
4. Industry *versus* Inferiority (5 to 16 years)
5. Identity *versus* Confusion (15 years to late twenties/early thirties)
6. Intimacy *versus* Isolation (18 to 40 years)

In theory each of these six stages builds on the successful negotiation of the previous stage, and ultimately leads to the creation of a whole, healthy and autonomous human being. According to this theory . . .

---

*Erikson's is not the only model of personality development, nor is it a theoretical rubber-stamp model that can be rigidly applied to both men and women. Nevertheless it is a theory that provides for an open-ended perspective of human development and one that despite its male gender bias, does define identity as an evolving process. Thus the redeeming quality of Erikson's model is that the journey toward self is seen as a process of working and reworking the earlier stages of development. These stages are common to both sexes and their search for identity.

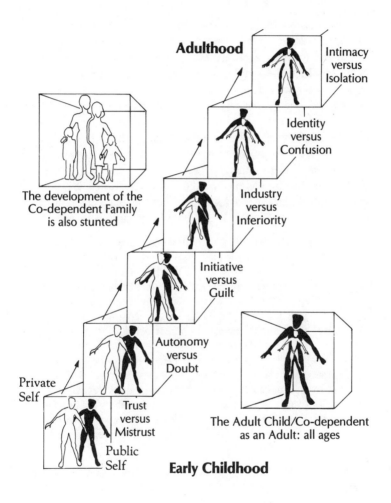

Adulthood

Intimacy
versus
Isolation

Identity
versus
Confusion

The development of the
Co-dependent Family
is also stunted

Industry
versus
Inferiority

Initiative
versus
Guilt

Autonomy
versus
Doubt

Private
Self

Trust
versus
Mistrust

The Adult Child/Co-dependent
as an Adult: all ages

Public
Self

Early Childhood

Figure 5.1 Early Childhood Developmental Model

The manner in which the individual copes — and his
chances for success — with each developmental crisis is dependent on the residual attitudes or orientations he has toward
himself and the world as a result of the way in which he dealt
with each of the previous tasks.

Clearly each of these six stages plays an important role in our
overall development, and we will take a closer look at each stage
in the next chapter. Most experts agree, however, that *trust* is the
point at which the whole process begins. Working from this assumption, researchers and clinicians alike have poured a great deal
of time and energy into trying to identify exactly what the specific
components of trust development are. Research seems to suggest
that there is a strong correlation between successful trust development and the quality of our early parental bond, particularly the
relationship to our mother.

While reviewing some of the literature on trust development in
early childhood, I came across several articles that spoke directly to
this issue. David Morris's ideas (1982) were particularly apt:

> The depth of emotional closeness and responsiveness in the
> early childhood attachment bond (meaning trust) and later in
> intimate relationships is unique in a person's life history, No
> other kinds of relationships rival these two for importance.
>
> Although they are not the same, there is much about
> intimacy that is central to secure attachment (again meaning
> trust). Love, mutual regulation and emotional safety character-
> ize both. The main difference is that in the attachment rela-
> tionship, only the caregiver is expected to provide compro-
> mise, give-and-take, knowledge of the other and commitment,
> whereas in an intimate relationship both partners are. Intimacy
> is not an appropriate construct to use in describing the infant's
> capabilities. A baby is expected to provide cues as to his
> needs, not strength and commitment. It is the caregiver's task
> to fit herself to the baby's needs.

There is a clear and significant difference between the developmental competence of a child and that of his or her parents. Trust
development within the infant depends on the parents' ability to
provide the kind of relationship that models and reflects trust.

Morris's paper speaks mostly about the subject of attachment theory,
which is a separate construct from that of psycho-emotional development. But both theories emphasize the importance of trust and the
significant role that parents play in its formation. Morris acknowledges

the overlap between these two theories and emphasizes the fact that "children are not equipped to intellectually defend themselves against insensitive and/or intrusive parenting and that as a result of such parenting, the infant is left feeling frustrated and deprived."

However, he points out, "It is not the feeling of frustration or deprivation alone that causes children not to trust, but also the lack of social meaning that their feelings create." We should note that the word "infant" comes from the Latin *infans*, "unable to speak." Clearly infants lack not only the cognitive skills needed to work through the confusion of sick parenting behavior, they also lack the words to express their confusion.

Taking all these factors into account, Erikson suggests that exposure to such obtrusive parenting early in life . . .

> . . . Leads to an internal sense of self as unworthy of being cared for, especially when feeling most insecure and in need of care . . . under such conditions children are forced to make up their own reasons as to why their caregiver/s are not "coming through." . . . The child's inability to understand obtrusive parenting very often leads to self-blame, giving rise to anger that when turned inward is experienced as shame and depression. Feelings that later in life are displaced to others. . . . These children are likely to grow to be cautious and mistrustful of the accessibility and responsiveness of significant others.

The Broken Bonds Of Trust

What does all this mean?

It means that children are vulnerable to psychological misunderstandings that can seriously undermine their social and emotional growth. When these misunderstandings occur, the normal process of trust development is interrupted and replaced by an unhealthy logic that says, "It is not safe here. The world is a dangerous place. I cannot trust anyone to be there for me. It is not okay to be needy and I am on my own."

Over time the child's private logic of mistrust in others turns into a private logic of mistrust in him or herself. Together the broken bonds of trust in self and others sets the child up for a lifetime filled with free-floating anxiety, self-doubt, fear, guilt and shame. In adulthood such unresolved emotional issues manifest themselves in all sorts of self-defeating behaviors that keep the human spirit from reaching its full potential or achieving real closeness with others.

> *For healthy interpersonal and intrapersonal develop-ment, trust is a must!*

Understanding Identity

I am a firm believer in the concept of process. I see it as the only realistic way to approach the question of identity development. Please keep in mind as you go through this chapter that identity is not etched in stone: It is a process, and you have a choice.

Trust Versus Mistrust

Where does the stage of trust development begin? Some say it begins at birth; others believe it begins while we are still in our mother's womb. Most experts agree that by the time we reach age one and a half we have already come to a basic sense of trust or mistrust in ourselves and others.

This is kind of scary when you consider all the different things that could happen to upset the delicate developmental balance of someone that age. The most critical factor during this period is our relationship with our parents, usually our mother. The developmental task of this first stage in life is to form a healthy bond of trust with a loving and nurturing adult who is capable of caring for us in a clear and consistent fashion.

We need an adult who can interact with us in a manner that is not confusing or threatening. We do not need someone who is verbally abusive, physically abusive, neglectful or unresponsive. If we get treated in any or all of these ways, we learn that it is not safe to be with our parent and that it is not okay to be needy. If these patterns continue, we will learn not to trust in the world or in ourselves.

The most difficult part is that at age one, we are not capable of sorting out the emotional confusion these dysfunctional messages create inside our spirit. At this stage life is strictly either/or: If something feels bad, we go away from it. If something feels good, we try to get more of it.

We are not supposed to have to take care of ourselves in a relationship with a parent. So when we feel that is the only way to get our needs met, we learn that love is a conditional reality. If we want love from our primary caregivers — and we do — then we learn by trial and error how to get them to come through for us. At the same time we are learning to get love through manipulation, we are also learning that love is a conditional reality and that we cannot count on being loved unless we have done something to earn it.

More than that, we have already begun to mistrust ourselves as people worth loving. So even when love comes without a price tag attached to it, we do not accept it. We say to ourselves privately, "If they ever found out who I really am, they would not love me, so I have to leave them before they leave me."

Clearly these thoughts are too sophisticated for the mind of an infant to unravel, but the seeds of emotional mistrust remain. What the child *feels* is really what the child *thinks*. Therefore our basic sense of trust is something that started out as a feeling. Such a feeling (as we will see in the later stages) not only becomes a thought but a personal *belief*.

Gender Differences

Trust *versus* Mistrust is the simplest stage to discuss in terms of gender differences and similarities. First, while the messages concerning trust are different for little boys and little girls, the underlying effect is the same. When the messages they receive during their first year of life say that it is not safe to trust in themselves or others, then the balance of their developmental journey will be tainted.

For example because of our longstanding history of chauvinistic attitudes among both male and female parents, it is likely that little girls are being made to feel "less than" little boys right from the start. How this devaluing message gets passed on may not be so easy to track down, but the fact that it does get passed on seems clear.

Could it be that our mothers were the primary senders of such a message or is it our fathers? Chances are it's both: moms who feel "less than" themselves and fathers who believe themselves that little girls are not as important as little boys. As a man with four daughters, the very idea that I would ever be the messenger of such a message hurts my heart.

The sad truth is that right from the start men are given a more positive — though not necessarily more healthy — set of messages. Worth measured by sex is an age-old form of discrimination that needs to be rooted out of the culture, out of the family and out of our spirit.

Autonomy Versus Doubt

You and I were meant to begin the process of moving away from our parents around the age of one. At this critical stage in our developmental journey we were all supposed to be busy learning the basics of autonomy — walking, talking, using the toilet. Through the mastery of these rudimentary skills we were then supposed to begin moving away from our primary caregivers, exploring our environment and practicing how to say no-no to our toys, no to our pets, no to our brothers and sisters, no to ourselves and — most risky of all — no to our parents.

Like learning to be successful at walking, talking and potty training, learning to say no required a great deal of understanding, support and love from our parents. Unfortunately these commodities are often in short supply in a troubled home. Many of us learned instead that we were somehow wrong for wanting to explore our space without constant ordering and direction from our parents. Through our unsuccessful attempts to do so we discovered that autonomy had an emotional price tag of shame attached to it. Moreover we learned that we could not trust in our own ability to exist separately from our parents.

Allen Sroufe, an expert in the area of early childhood development, believes that the quality of early adaptation influences adaptation with respect to later developmental issues and that a secure parental attachment supports confidence in exploration. This in turn, he asserts, encourages the development of autonomy in the second year of life by preparing the toddler to tolerate firm limits without feeling his or her security and sense of self-trust is jeopardized.

Most developmentalists feel that we come to a sense of our own autonomy through a process of trial and error, reward and punishment. Consequently, when the limits we experience during the first to third year of life are inconsistent, rigid and unfair, we start to doubt in ourselves as people. We do not simply believe that we have *done* something wrong, which is guilt, we come to believe that there *is* something wrong with us, which is shame.

In the developmental order of things, our inability to establish a clear sense of autonomy forces us to remain the helpless and dependent child. Instead of learning a confident, straightforward and spontaneous style of relating to self and others, we have learned to be anxious, manipulative and tentative.

Our parents' failure to understand our needs, set healthy limits and help us negotiate a functional sense of autonomy left us to wonder: "Am I capable of being alone? Can I be who I really am? Is there something wrong with me?"

It took me until my early 30s to understand that I had the ability to be alone with myself, and that there was nothing wrong with who I was. Up until that time I did not like being with me and I avoided being alone at all costs. The very idea of having to be alone with myself sent me into an acute state of depression. Of course, I knew that I was not supposed to feel the way I did, but being the son of a chronically stoic father I was far too proud to say anything about myself. Real men were not supposed to be afraid. So, like most people who operate from a position of doubt and shame, I worked hard to portray myself as a man in total control of his life. No task was too great, no request too small. I could handle it all — alone.

I would do almost anything to keep from being alone. The strangest thing about this was that I found myself involved with people I didn't really like and circumstances I wanted no part of. Ironically my efforts to medicate my loneliness only served to make it worse. Eventually it got so bad that I could hardly face the idea of having to go back to my own apartment alone. Even sleep became an enemy.

As my fear of loneliness progressed I became more and more dependent on others for my good feelings. I became a raging people-pleaser in an effort to gain approval and acceptance. I spent an inordinate amount of time feeling anxious about my relationships and worried incessantly about how others saw me. I was convinced that in my doing for others, others would do for me.

Lord, did I have a lot to learn!

My lack of autonomy made it impossible for me to say no or to set healthy boundaries. Without realizing it, I had become a victim of my own delusion. I was trapped in what I call a "developmental time warp" — a kind of suspended animation where physical and mental growth continues, but social, psychological and emotional growth is stunted. In other words — co-dependency.

Whatever we call it, the end result of our continued inability to establish a healthy sense of autonomy is always the same.

Our Unhealthy Autonomy

1. We have problems saying no.
2. We have problems being alone.
3. We have problems doing things alone.
4. We have problems making commitments.
5. We have problems setting healthy boundaries.
6. We have problems leaving unhealthy relationships.
7. We have problems making decisions.
8. We have problems with inadequacy.
9. We have problems with self-doubt.
10. We have problems with shame.

Gender Differences

We can use the list above to explore some of the different gender issues of Autonomy *versus* Doubt:

1. Men say no and they get respect. Women say no and they are called bitches.
2. A woman struggles with being alone because she is lonely. Men struggle with being alone because they are bored.
3. Women have problems doing things alone because they feel an absence when they're not relating to someone. Men struggle with doing things alone because they're worried about how it looks and about what others might think.
4. Women have problems making commitments because they do not feel good enough about themselves. Men have problems making commitments because they might be abandoned or taken advantage of.

5. Women do not set healthy boundaries because they fear people might not like them. Men do not set healthy boundaries because they get in the way and cramp their style.
6. Women stay in unhealthy relationships because they believe that they can change people or because they have given so much of themselves to the other person, they do not feel strong enough to leave. Men stay in unhealthy relationships because they feel guilty about leaving and worry that the other person will not survive.
7. Men have problems making decisions because they are afraid of making a mistake and looking stupid. Women have difficulty making decisions because they are worried about making a mistake and hurting someone's feelings.
8. Men have problems feeling inadequate when they do not have a job or something to do that they are good at. Women have problems with feeling inadequate when they do not have a primary relationship or close friends to identify with.
9. Men have problems with self-doubt in relationship to their physical or mental capabilities. Women have self-doubt with respect to their emotional and interpersonal relationship capabilities.
10. Men have problems with shame in respect to mental and physical shortcomings. Women have problems with shame in respect to emotional and physical shortcomings.

It is in this stage that the primary developmental differences in the identity theme of men and women begin to surface. Men, it seems, are more *intra*personally preoccupied; women are more *inter*personally preoccupied. The covert (unspoken) and overt (spoken) message in our culture says that men achieve autonomy by being able to do for themselves, and that women achieve autonomy by being able to do for others. The result is a developmental dichotomy of the sexes whereby men are looking in one direction to get their needs met and women are looking in the other.

Initiative Versus Guilt

The next stage of child development is what Erikson calls *initiative*. During this third stage of our progression toward adulthood, we are supposed to be learning how to use our imagination and exercise our own discretion with respect to basic problem-solving.

The primary question of this stage is, "Why?" Why are things the way they are? Why is grass green? Why are there clouds? Why does it rain? Why do we have to go to bed? Why is Mommy crying? Why does Daddy drink? Why do Mom and Dad fight all the time? And why do they yell at me?

From this early wondering, which begins around the age of three and a half to four, we start forming our own ideas of how things work and why, how we relate to the world and how the world relates to us and what the difference between right and wrong feels like. When the answers we receive in response to our questions are unclear and fail to make sense, our imagination takes over and we begin to create our own meaning. "There are monsters under my bed."

Due to our underdeveloped sense of ego-resilience (the ability not to internalize outside events) and our lack of intellectual prowess (the ability to accurately define and resolve abstract problems) we hypothesize that somehow we are responsible for why things happen and that we are somehow to blame.

For example, we conclude that Dad drinks because Mom is always upset and Mom is always upset because we do not always do what we are told. Therefore it must be our fault that they do not get along.

The inevitable result of such distorted thinking is that we become overly responsible and develop an unrealistic view of our ability to control things. Intellectually we come to think of ourselves as people responsible for how others feel and act; agents who are responsible *for* rather than *to* others.

When the external realities of our everyday life get out of hand, we feel guilty and afraid. Our internal sense of emotional well-being becomes dependent on receiving the validation of others — our parents, our spouse, our children, our friends, our boss, our next-door neighbor. We see everyone but ourselves as capable.

The harder we try to manage our insides by managing the outside, the more dependent we become. Inevitably our approval-seeking only results in more of what we had been trying to avoid in the first place: rejection, abandonment and guilt.

With each failure we become more and more convinced that we are incapable of doing for ourselves and that to try is to fail. Eventually the very idea of doing for ourselves leads to a feeling of guilt. Finally we lose all of our emotional perspective and end up feeling guilty for things we had nothing to do with: Mom's depression, Dad's drinking, sister's suicide, brother's sexual abuse — or, if you're *really* feeling guilty, the war-torn Middle East and the starving children in Africa.

Even in lieu of overwhelming evidence to the contrary, we continue to judge ourselves mercilessly and persist in our efforts to manage the unmanageable. Fueled by feelings of unhealthy guilt and shame, we start feeding ourselves sick messages: "If only I had tried harder. If only I had been more patient. If only I had been a little smarter . . . *then* things would have turned out better."

Like our loss of trust and autonomy, our loss of initiative only serves to divide us further from ourselves. Lacking the ability to act independently of outside influences, our own individuality becomes confused to the point that we lose all sense of where we end and others begin.

Here's a short list of symptoms related to lack of initiative:

1. We have trouble asking for help.
2. We have problems with rigidity.
3. We fear making mistakes.
4. We lack spontaneity.
5. We have feelings of unhealthy guilt.
6. We tend to be overly suspicious.
7. We are evasive.
8. We are externally focused.
9. We have problems with inappropriate caretaking.
10. We have problems with irresponsibility and procrastination.

Gender Differences

Based on the list above, here are some gender differences for the stage of Initiative *Versus* Guilt:

1. Asking for help is a problem for men because it is a sign of weakness, a quality unbecoming to the male stereotype. Women have problems asking for help because they feel unworthy and undeserving.
2. Men's problem with rigidity seems to center on their fear of losing control of their cutting edge — physically, psychologically or emotionally — particularly as it relates to their job, family and social standing. Women, on the other hand, tend to demonstrate more of a rigidity with respect to home, friends, spouse and family, things that are central to their intrapersonal well-being.
3. Women fear making mistakes because they do not want to do anything that might hurt others or damage their relationships. Men tend to fear making mistakes because they do not wish to appear ignorant, incompetent, stupid or foolish.

4. Women have problems with spontaneity because they fear judgment, rejection or relationship abandonment. Men have problems with spontaneity because they fear appearing foolish.
5. Men experience guilt when they initiate something or invest themselves and no one cares, or when they fail to initiate or invest themselves and someone confronts them on it. Women tend to experience guilt when they initiate period. In the co-dependent extreme women should be submissive, helpless and passive.
6. Women tend to be suspicious of people's intentions and real motives with respect to social or interpersonal relationships. Men tend to be more suspicious with respect to career or financial issues.
7. Women are generally more evasive about interpersonal thoughts and feelings. Men are generally more evasive about intrapersonal thoughts and feelings.
8. Men tend to focus externally on their relationship to things. Women tend to focus externally on their relationship to people.
9. Women tend to be emotional and moral caretakers. Men tend to be intellectual and organizational caretakers.
10. Men tend to be more interpersonally irresponsible — they fail to initiate meaningfully on a one-to-one basis. Women tend to be more intrapersonally irresponsible — they fail to initiate meaningfully within themselves. Men tend to be intrapersonally selfish; women tend to be interpersonally selfless.

Despite the disparities between men and women in this stage of their developmental struggle, both sexes experience an equally profound sense of guilt and self-doubt over their respective shortcomings in this area. Women generally have a harder time in the arena of intrapersonal initiative, while men seem to have a harder time with interpersonal initiative. The consequences, however, are basically the same: the creation of unhealthy guilt, an increased sense of self-doubt and a diminished sense of self-worth.

Industry Versus Inferiority

During this stage of our journey toward adulthood, around the age of four, our primary task is to develop a sense of confidence and pride in our ability to make healthy choices and finish what we start. It is also during this stage that we begin to learn the basics of healthy problem-solving. Through a combination of verbal and behavioral examples our parents model for us the rules of both social etiquette and moral conduct.

If the limits that our parents set for us during this period are rigid and controlling, then instead of industry we learn inferiority. The task of setting healthy goals, learning self-direction, defining social and moral boundaries, practicing problem-resolution skills and developing a more sophisticated understanding of the world are all part of this stage of a child's life.

Failure to resolve these conflicts, according to Erikson, results in feelings of inferiority and futility. In our adulthood these feelings are reflected in the following seeming inabilities:

1. We are unable to complete projects.
2. We are unable to set realistic goals.
3. We are unable to enlist appropriate help.
4. We are unable to be flexible.
5. We are unable to deal with loss.
6. We are unable to share problems.
7. We are unable to handle criticism.
8. We are unable to learn from experience.
9. We are unable to handle conflict.
10. We are unable to let go of old ideas.

The healthy inner voice of industry is a parental voice that guides and directs the child in our spirit in a kind, loving, compassionate and caring fashion. This affirming parental voice says, "I love you. I believe in you. I am glad you are with me. I'll always be there for you. You have a right to be."

Through good times and bad, it is the job of the parent in us to stand by our inner child and send these healthy messages. In whatever verbal or behavioral form we choose to express these supportive messages to our inner child, they should *always* come from an unconditional understanding that children are perfect.

In contrast to these healthy parental messages that serve to promote a sense of self-confidence in the child's abilities to see a project through, there are always those messages that only serve to promote unhealthy feelings of incompetence and inferiority in the child: "You are a stupid, obstinate, self-centered, spoiled little brat. . . . When are you ever going to grow up? . . . You can't seem to do anything right."

These abusive, punishing and angry parental messages are the most dysfunctional part of our intrapersonal struggle and cause the most psychological and emotional damage to our spirit. They are the servants of shame that says, "I am flawed," and the pillars of a child's fear that says, "I am not capable."

Gender Differences

When it comes to the problem of industry, both men and women share the same intellectual profile. Both are invested in an intrapersonal belief system that says:

1. If I succeed, they are only going to expect more out of me, and I don't think I can handle more.
2. What I do is never good enough, so why bother?
3. I should be able to do this alone.
4. Everyone has their own problems and I don't want to be a burden.
5. If I ask them for help, I'll be indebted to them.
6. If you want it done right, you have to do it yourself.
7. Everyone's a critic, so you might as well leave them out of it.
8. It doesn't matter how hard I try, it always turns out the same.
9. If I open my mouth, it's only going to create more problems.
10. Doing it this way was good enough for my folks and it's good enough for me.

These thoughts and feelings are equal-opportunity problems. They do not discriminate on the basis of age, race, sexual orientation, gender, religion or national origin. It is nice to know that men and women are the same in some respects. Now if only there were more of an androgynous blending of the developmental strengths between men and women, we would be in a lot better shape than we are now.

Identity Versus Identity Confusion And Intimacy Versus Isolation

Unlike the previous stages, which remain fixed in their developmental relationship to one another, the final two stages do not. According to Morris,

> Despite Erikson's presentation of the phase of Identity *Versus* Identity Confusion as preceding the phase of Intimacy *Versus* Isolation, his clinical writings emphasize the reciprocal inter-

digitation (interaction) of the two struggles in normal development. In short, the more you know about yourself, the closer
you can get to another person, and the best way for learning
about yourself is close encounter.

For this reason I believe it would be most helpful to conclude this
section with an integrated discussion of the remaining two stages.

What Do We Mean By Identity

When we possess a sense of *identity,* we possess a clear sense of
who and what we are which is separate from others; we are emotionally and intellectually independent; we are emancipated from
dependency on the outside world for a sense of self and we possess
realistic understanding of our intrapersonal strengths and weak-
nesses. A sense of identity means that we have developed a clear,
loving, accepting, and intimate relationship with ourselves.

By Erikson's standards there is no perfect or rigidly definable
outcome in our search for identity. Rather he suggests that our
search for identity is an ongoing process that continues to be refined
throughout the balance of our adult lives. This open-ended search
ultimately results in a clear sense of intrapersonal integrity, self-
respect and life resolution. Our task, then, during the Identity *Versus*
Confusion stage, is to sort out the wheat from the chaff, make peace
with ourselves and become one with ourselves.

The catch is that in order for us to truly know ourselves, we must
first successfully resolve the basic issues of trust, autonomy, initiative
and industry. For those of us who enter our adult years without these
basic skills, the search for identity is likely to be a frustrating experience laced with feelings of confusion, despair, guilt and shame.

What Do We Mean By Intimacy

Erikson defines intimacy as "the capacity to commit one's self to
a concrete affiliation and/or partnership and to develop the ethical
strength to abide by such commitments, even though they may call
for significant sacrifices and compromises."

The underlying assumption in this definition is that intimacy rests
on a foundation of basic trust, autonomy, initiative, industry and
identity. In short, the experience of intimacy presupposes that both
parties are capable of participating on a close interpersonal basis
without compromising the integrity of their own intrapersonal relationship. Intimacy, then, is not an appropriate term to use when

describing a relationship between two people who lack a fundamental sense of self separate from others — that is, co-dependents.*

The Intimate Paradox

Failure to negotiate the perilous stages of intimacy and identity leave us in a peculiar predicament. We are unable to experience intimacy, yet we persist in trying to form relationships. We are in deep water.

According to Jacob Orlofsky, "Failure at this task is reflected in repeated withdrawal from close relationships, self-absorption and a deep sense of isolation."

Now we're trying to keep from drowning. According to Morris, in our search for the "secure base," we become "oversensitive to frustration . . . ego-brittle . . . an ego-overcontroller or undercontroller." What does that mean? It means that our ego, our sense of "I," is on pretty shaky ground.

As a result we go one of two ways. Morris defines an ego-overcontroller as "one who tends to be rigid and preservative . . . to delay gratification to the point of self-deprivation . . . to be self-restrictive." An ego-undercontroller, on the other hand, "tends to be spontaneous, to lack impulse control, to be unable to delay gratification . . . to have difficulty with purposive behavior." Sound familiar?

About ego-brittle individuals, Morris continues,

> They may be occupied with competitiveness, preference for self-definition vis-a-vis authority figures, and experimentation with this effect on others by aggressiveness and sexuality. He/she has internalized a self-representation as undeserving and dependent and, unless circumstances in the caregiver's life change to provide for an increase in emotional ability and an increase in tolerance for protest and stored-up anger, these youngsters will have difficulty successfully negotiating later interpersonal crises, especially intimacy.
>
> They may eventually defend against their sense of vulnerability and shame by a protective shell of invulnerability, stereotyped roles and an outward posture of exaggerated pride . . . Another, paradoxical but expected outcome for the anxiously attached child is that he/she would continue to experience considerable emotional hunger and would, as a result, continue to seek out relationships as a format for reworking issues of basic trust.

Intimacy is also not an appropriate term to use when discussing the relationship between two children or between child and parent.

In much of the traditional literature and research on child development, this profile is often called a "dependent personality" profile. It is, however, not so much a trait (symptom) perspective of dependency as it is an implied personal belief system. This system compels us to act as if self-worth, energy, purpose and direction all come from sources outside ourselves.

According to Virginia Satir, the theoretical premise behind dependency stresses that "a person's psychological makeup, especially that which has to do with identity and intimacy, is best understood as an implicit set of expectations that guides one to recognize, seek out, create and maintain social situations that confirm their sense of self-unity."

Some of the best-known family systems theorists of our time — Bowen, Haley and Satir, to name just a few — have long suggested that dependency problems in childhood and later in adulthood are (aside from genetic influences in personality) the direct result of dysfunctional parenting patterns that call upon children to act as either partner or parent to an adult caregiver who is acting like a child. Satir says that . . .

> The blurring of the traditional boundaries between parent and child is seen as a causal antecedent to later dependency. Moreover, it is assumed that without some corrective or therapeutic re-alignment of these relationship boundaries, the patterns . . . are likely to get passed on from one generation to the next.

Drawing on this basic assumption Morris concludes that:

> The dependent belief system precludes true intimacy as well as true autonomy because getting too vulnerable can result in a fearful feeling of fusion and lack of self-control. It is as if the person will not risk intimacy because internally they do not feel like the other will "come through" for them. Healthy intimate relationships are avoided, since the expectations and demands of normal close relationships are likely to be felt as confinement, control and domination.

From a developmental point of view, it is perfectly clear that dependency-type behavior is not characteristic of a person who has achieved a clear identity. Nor through a process of logical deduction would it be characteristic of someone who had achieved true intimacy with another. Paradoxically it is one's inability to build and maintain a close intimate relationship that reveals one's lack of identity.

People who have no identity are in a perpetual state of panic. Since they can't find anyone inside, they look for identity outside — seeking to take other's identities for their own. According to Erikson, they have three choices: "isolation, stereotyped relations or intimacy with 'improbable partners' in an attempt to delineate the 'fuzzy outlines of identity.' "

So what kind of partners do such people end up with? Bowlby paints this chilling picture:

> A dependent person in search of a mate is likely to seek out someone who is equally needy and to assimilate that person to this self-representation, instead of perceiving them as they actually are . . . It is as if they are orbiting around each other, both imagining that the other is stationary. A pseudo-intimacy or tandem isolation develops.

Satir continues this line of thought, expressed by David Morris:

> More dysfunctional people tend to be driven toward people who can serve as extensions of themselves, a format for working out unresolved and recurring conflicts. The initial attraction is sustained by the self-esteem enhancing effects of being in love. When that fades and disappointments appear, they each begin maneuvers to try to change the other into what they had hoped for (a secure base) without chasing the other away. The disappointments and subsequent manipulations increase the spouses' frustration and anger. Characteristic of anxious attachment, anger is experienced as a threat to the security of the relationship and its expression is avoided. Faced with declining self-esteem as mates, the tension finds a course in triangulating another into the relationship. Many "others are used, such as in-laws, chemicals, concern of diet, work, lovers, but the best other is a child, since children serve parents so well as a vehicle of the extension of self." [*Figure 6-1 illustrates this sort of co-dependent identity issue in addiction.*]

The experience of intimacy and the experience of co-dependency are about as incompatible as oil and water. Nonetheless a strong negative correlation exists between them. Where one is present, the other is conspicuously absent. In this instance where there is co-dependency, there is no intimacy; and where there is intimacy, there is no co-dependency.

Equally perplexing are the contradictory and yet paradoxical similarities these two terms share. For example, there is the traditional view of intimacy, which very often suggests an outward demeanor of meekness and vulnerability. In fact, however, the ability to be truly

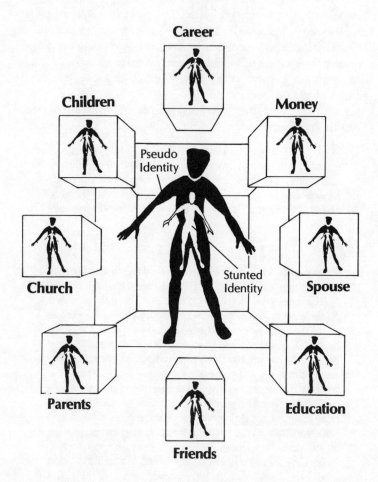

Figure 6.1. Issue Addiction

Adult children and co-dependents become addicted to outside
issues in order to medicate their feelings, avoid conflict, find acceptance and a sense of self. The result is a pseudo identity that says . . .
"I am who I know, who I marry, how much money I make, what
religion I am, what kind of car I drive, who my parents are, what
degree I hold, or what type of work I do." For these people the truth
is . . . If they are what they do and then they don't, they aren't.
These outside projections of identity for the co-dependent make
intimacy with self and others impossible.

intimate requires an underlying strength and self-confidence. Co-dependency, on the other hand, which often reflects an outward appearance of strength and self-confidence, is actually a sophisticated external cover-up for a serious internal lack of these very qualities.

Consequently it would be a serious contradiction in terms to suggest that a person who was caught up in the maze of co-dependency could actually maintain a lasting intimate relationship with anyone. Ironically there are probably millions of adults who have tried and failed at intimacy precisely because they are co-dependent.

Clearly when one out of every two marriages in this country fails, something is very wrong. A 50 percent failure rate is hardly the kind of statistic that inspires one's confidence in the Great American Dream.

Now don't misunderstand me — I do not mean to suggest that co-dependency is the sole cause of divorce in America. But I do believe that it plays a significant part. Certainly we can ill afford to underestimate the destructive power of this dis-ease, particularly when it has so much to do with our own inner bond of intimacy.

Relatively Speaking

Childhood is not guaranteed to be happy and trouble-free. In fact the odds of reaching adulthood without experiencing some sort of emotional, psychological or physical trauma are slim to none. Nevertheless it is a serious mistake to minimize the impact of our past as it relates to our future. Pain is relative. It should never be measured against the experience of others.

The very idea that our pain does not count because someone else has suffered more is a sick rationalization. We are the sum total of our experience. And in order for us to successfully resolve our identity, we must be willing to make room for the whole of those experiences. To do otherwise is to abandon oneself and end up living a life by omission — that is, a co-dependent life. No one who tries to cope with their past by editing it will ever come to know themselves in an intimate way.

Who Is Riding On Your Bus?

For millions of people the experiences of childhood were anything but positive. For example, an estimated 30 million people in this country are children of alcoholics, and another 15 or 20 million grew up in other types of troubled homes. No wonder there has been such a groundswell of interest in the subject of adult children and co-dependency.

It is purely speculation on my part, but I would be willing to guess that there is a positive correlation between the number of divorces in this country over the past ten years and the number of adult child/ co-dependents who got married during that same period. I would also venture to guess that in more than half of these broken marriages either one or both parties had been married at least once before.

The emotional and psychological fallout of a troubled family history is not likely to go away just because we somehow managed to survive it. Healing the wounds of a troubled past requires more than just survival. We must stop pretending that we know who we are, stop trying to outrun the past, let go of our emotional enmesh-ments, emancipate ourselves from our family of origin and begin to look at our family within.

In many respects our inner family is a composite of our nuclear and extended families. Significant people — parents, grandparents, siblings, aunts and uncles — ultimately become the prototypes for the different members of our intrapersonal family. In many in-stances these folks were at the core of our pain and suffering. Despite this fact we continue to carry them around as passengers on our psychic and emotional bus.

And these are not nice passengers! They are angry, guilty and shaming passengers who like to prey on the innocence of our inner child, using him or her as a dumping ground for all their unmet expectations and bad feelings. They are cowardly critics who deny the past, hide from the present and worry about tomorrow. And because they have one foot in the past and one foot in the future, they end up dumping their baggage all over the present.

Are these really the kind of people you want to carry on your bus?

Defiant? Who? Me?

Over the last 15 years I have come to know my inner family well. Before then, however, I only knew that occasionally I would expe-rience these strange conversations in my head. I wasn't hearing voices, you understand — that would have been another diagnosis all together! These were just self-talk voices, the kind we all hear when we're trying to work something out.

> *SELF-TALK:*
> *Self-talk is a normal and necessary part of maintaining a healthy relationship with yourself. That old rule that says "People who talk to themselves are crazy" is just so much tripe. The truth is that the people who do not talk to themselves are either dead or in a state of suspended animation.*

So I would be trucking along, doing my own thing and trying to mind my own business, when suddenly something would trigger off one of those internal skirmishes. It didn't take much — just about anything would do.

For example, one day I was talking to one of my colleagues about something that had happened at work. For some reason he suddenly changed the subject and confronted me on my having been late for a meeting that morning. Instantly I got defensive, as was my style back then, and started talking to myself. Intellectually I knew that he had a right to his opinion, but that's not what I was telling myself inside. My self-talk went something like this: *"This guy is trying to make me look stupid. Yeah, who does he think he is anyway. He's not exactly Mr. Perfect himself. He's just jealous of me. No one has the right to talk to us that way! We don't have to take this kind of crap from him. Just blow him off. He's nobody."*

I didn't know who was saying what or to whom, but I had heard enough. It was all the unhealthy provocation I needed. And without giving it another thought I verbally let him have it with both barrels.

I could feel myself unloading things on him that had no relevance whatsoever to what he had been talking about. I was beside myself. I wanted to stop but I couldn't. I felt like a little kid who had just been caught doing something wrong and was trying to get out of it by throwing a tantrum. I had regressed from a competent adult to an over-reacting and defiant child.

The whole incident reminded me of the way I used to lose it with my dad. I had managed to turn this guy into another authority figure whom I felt I needed to dethrone. I kept dumping on him until finally he just threw up his arms in frustration, turned his back on me, and walked away. He must have thought I was crazy. I really was out of it. So much so, in fact, that when it was all over I couldn't even remember what had got me so riled up in the first place.

As my head cleared and I started to come back to my senses, I was hit with the usual amount of dripping guilt and shame — shilt again — not unlike the way I used to feel after coming off a heavy bout of drinking. The worst part was that I didn't even have drinking as an excuse for what I had done.

Well, as they say, what goes around comes around. If you keep running people over, one day someone is going to run over you. My AA sponsor, Walt H., was particularly good at doing this to me. After witnessing one of the more colorful episodes in my career, he came to me and said, "You know, Bob, you're really a defiant man."

The defensive child in me shot back, "No, I'm not!"

And Walt said, "Yes, you are."

And I said, "No, I am *not* being defiant. I am being *assertive!*"

You see, in my four years as a treatment counselor — and I use the term loosely — I had learned lots of new clinical terms to use to excuse my behavior: "I'm not angry, I'm *agitated.* I'm not being rude, I'm being *honest.* I'm not being sarcastic, I'm being *graphic.*" Like so many adult child/co-dependents who have the knowledge but no real understanding, I had become more sophisticated at being dysfunctional.

Fortunately my sponsor had enough knowledge and understanding to see through all my intellectual games and cut to the chase. So Walt replied, "No, Bob, you're not being assertive, you're being defiant. If you don't want to listen to me, you don't have to. But if you want to learn something for a change, then sit down, keep your mouth shut and listen."

My sponsor had just challenged me to sit down, shut up and learn something. By itself this probably wouldn't have been enough to get my attention, so he hooked me with my guilt:

Walt: I'm your sponsor, right? And when you asked me to be your sponsor, you made a commitment to me that you would do your part, right? You promised that if I ever came to you with something I thought you needed to hear that you would at least hear me out, right?

Me: Okay! Okay! I'm listening. You don't have to guilt me anymore.

Guilt, especially *healthy* guilt, has been given a bad rap in recent years. There *is* such a thing as healthy guilt. It is the kind of guilt that helps us recognize when we are violating some moral value or ethical standard. The basic problem with guilt is not that we have it, but that we do not always know when to feel it. For example, there is a big difference between the kind of healthy guilt that I would feel when my sponsor confronted me on a point of law, and the *un*healthy guilt I felt as a child who believed my mother's alcoholism was my fault.

The kind of guilt Walt H. used to hook me was the kind that we should have when we're doing something that compromises our relationship to self or others. He knew exactly how to do this without having to shame me. I guess that's why I trusted him so much and why I allowed him to talk to me the way he did.

Walt was a healthy man who confronted people with love and respect. He never spoke to me directly about the various members of my inner family, but he always seemed to have an intuitive understanding about them and a method of communicating that spoke to all three dimensions. He seemed to sense their presence and knew exactly how to get their attention. For instance, in a three-dimensional translation of his communication Walt might have sounded like this:

Walt: Excuse me, son, I'm not talking to your child right now, I'm talking to your adult and parent. So you just sit down over here until I'm done. I love you and everything is going to be all right. And yes, I love the parent and adult in you too. Unfortunately I can't say the same for their behavior. Frankly I think it stinks to high heaven, and it's time that I said something to them about it.

That's pretty much the way I think it might have gone if he had been using an inner family model of talking. We'll take a closer look at this three-dimensional style of communication as we go on. For now we'll continue with the dialogue as it was.

Walt: Good. I'm glad you're listening, Bob, because I'm only going to say this to you once.

Walt was a patient man, but never one to mince words. So I knew when he said he was only going to say it once, he meant it. I was glad that he talked to me as a man and not as a child, but it also scared me. Whenever he decided that it was time for one of his little talks, I always knew that I was going to be hit with a brick wrapped in a pillow. *Bam!* "Do I have your attention, Bob?"

I could see it coming, but I had made a commitment to listen and, as I said, I trusted the man. He put his hand on my shoulder — that was the pillow — and then he let me have it.

Walt: Bob, the word 'defiance' means to live in the world without faith. And you, my friend, are the epitome of someone who has no faith.

Me: [Ouch! The brick!]

Walt: It hurts me to say this, Bob, but in the two years that I have been your sponsor, I have yet to see you demonstrate any real faith. Not in me — and I'm your sponsor, the man you said you picked because you trusted him.

Not in your AA group, which you credit with having given you a second chance.

Not in your friends, whom you say you trust with your life.

Not in your Higher Power, whom you say you invited into your life.

And, worst of all, not even faith in yourself.

You have the belief, but you do not have the faith. And that is the source of your defiance.

I love you, Bob, and I want you to understand what it is that I am trying to tell you. I want you to realize that there is a big difference between just having a belief and having faith in it. Lord knows, it took me a long time to learn this lesson. But today I can honestly say I have both. I do not just believe that my Higher Power loves me, I count on it.

I once heard a story that really helped we with my defiance. Maybe it would help you too.

Once there was a young boy who went to the circus and saw a tightrope walker dancing across a high wire and pushing a small red wheelbarrow. It was the most amazing thing the boy had ever seen. He was so taken by the spectacle that he came every night for a week to see this man perform. By the seventh day the little boy had *come to believe* that the man would always be able to make the crossing.

Then, on the last night, the tightrope walker yelled down to the crowd, "Is there anyone down there who would like to come up here with me and ride in my wheelbarrow?" Suddenly, a wave of paralyzing fear and doubt came over the boy. He thought the man was talking directly to him. The very idea of having to ride in the wheelbarrow scared the boy so badly that he dropped the bag of popcorn he'd been eating, got up out of his seat, and ran right out of the tent.

You're like that little boy, Bob. You believe that the tight-rope walker can take care of himself. But you do not have faith that he could take care of you.

He had done it again, just as I had predicted he would. A loaded pillow right upside the head. His message was loud and clear. Like a skilled surgeon with sharp knife, he'd managed to cut through all my sick defiance in one swift stroke.

I could not think of anything to say, so I tried to put on one of my best, "Who, me?" looks, hoping that he would let it go. He didn't, though. He just stared back. And then, in classic style, he put his arms around me, gave me a big AA-type hug, and said, "I love you, Bob."

I remembered thinking as he walked away how great it would have been if my own father would have parented me that way. Good parenting was hard enough to come by when I was a child, harder yet when I was an adult. Still, it was exactly what I needed: good parenting. As it turned out, Walt H. was the first of several surrogate parents in my life. He was not the last, but he was the most significant. And I will remember him with gratitude always.

AND NOW, A WORD ABOUT YOUR SPONSOR . . . I am a real believer in self-help and the idea of sponsorship. If by chance you do not have a 12-Step group or a sponsor, I strongly recommend that you get at least one of each.

If you have never been to a 12-Step self-help group — such as AA, Al-Anon, Overeaters Anonymous, Narcotics Anonymous, Adult Children of Alcoholics (ACoA), or Co-dependents Anonymous — you might not be familiar with the concept of a sponsor.

A sponsor is a person you choose to be your advocate and guide in your journey toward physical, emotional, psychological and spiritual recovery. Since you are picking this person to be a surrogate mentor and teacher to your inner parent, adult and child, he or she should already have gone where you have yet to go. This person must have a real handle on recovery and must not be afraid to challenge you when you are getting off the track.

My sponsor knew how to stand toe-to-toe with the defiant members of my inner family: my inner child, who was confused, mistrustful, angry, hurt, lonely, guilty and ashamed; my inner parent, who liked to play God, act morally superior, and beat up on the little child in my spirit; and my inner adult, who was constantly trying to intellectualize, analyze and pulverize away every part of my moral and emotional being.

How do you choose a sponsor? I'm not sure how I picked out Walt H. I think it was my inner child who picked him — he liked and hated the man. But Walt H. just felt like the right one. I know this isn't a lot to go on, but I believe that if you seek in earnest, you will recognize your sponsor. It is to your advantage to pick a sponsor of the same sex (or opposite sexual orientation). The last thing you need to end up with is a sponsor with whom you share sexual feelings. Sponsors must be objective, and a sponsor who wants to be your lover is incapable of objectivity.

Filling In
The Gaps

Because I was an angry, defiant, guilty and shameful person in my recovery, the lack of a healthy, loving *intra*personal parent was, to say the least, a serious problem. The real problem, however, was the combined lack of a healthy parent and adult within my spirit.

This lack was at the core of my defiance, and pointed back to those early years when as a result of my family's struggles, I failed to successfully resolve the basic developmental conflicts of trust, autonomy, initiative, industry and identity. These gaps in my developmental history made it difficult for me to be with myself. They invariably divided me from myself and caused me to build my identity from the outside in, instead of from the inside out. Such is the case for most adult child/co-dependents. These gaps in development give rise to an intrapersonal family whose members are confused about their roles and unable to live together in harmony.

Problems in development begin when the bond of trust between ourselves and our parents is broken. This shattered bond of trust starts the developmental ball rolling in the wrong directions and

81

turns our developmental energies outward rather than inward. The more dependent we become on the outside world — work, relationships, food, sex, alcohol — to fill up the internal void the further away we get from ourselves.

Ultimately this misguided logic and external co-dependent focus actually stunts our developmental growth, divides our intrapersonal life and creates what I call "the black hole in our soul."

The only way I know to correct this divisive co-dependent logic and recover our family within is to do the following:

1. Admit to ourselves that we cannot do it alone.
2. Break out of our isolation.
3. Ask for help.
4. Start sharing with ourselves and others what we really think and feel.
5. Begin to question who we are and what we are doing.
6. Take the risk to challenge our belief systems (that is, our logic, moral values and inner rules).
7. Work to develop a conscious understanding of the different members of our intrapersonal family (parent, adult and child).
8. Learn to identify who is talking and when.
9. Identify who is driving your bus.
10. Do not allow the child in our spirit to drive the bus.
11. Let the child have all of his or her thoughts and feelings.
12. Stop the adult in you from intellectualizing your feelings away and abandoning his or her responsibilities to validate the emotional side of your spirit.
13. Do not permit the parent in you to shame the child and abandon his or her responsibilities to nurture the child.
14. Teach the parent and adult that the child in you is not the one who needs to be fixed.
15. Help the parent and adult in you accept the fact that the child of your spirit is perfect and that all she or he really needs is a healthy inner adult and parent to provide and care for them.

This list may seem a bit overwhelming, but relax — I'm not suggesting you try to get through it in the next week, the next month or even the next year. It is a list of things that need to be addressed over the course of the next two or three years.

It is also helpful to remember that recovery is not a race, and that you are striving for progress, not perfection. I tried the hurry-up-and-get-it-together route, and I can tell you that it did not work. It took me almost 25 years to get as separated from myself as I was, and I learned that it takes some time to put it all back together.

The simple truth is that it takes time to *know* that it takes time. It has only taken me five short years to come this far, and I would do it all again to be where I am today. It's not such a long time, when I think about how long it took me to lose myself in the first place.

I believe that what holds true for me holds true for others like me. It is not the 200 meetings you attend, the number of counselors you see or the 65 self-help books you have read that ultimately make the difference. It is the accumulation of all these investments in recovery that makes the difference.

So have some faith and don't let your inner defiance and self-doubt hold you back. Difficult as it may be to believe, it won't take you as long to be found as it took you to get lost. It helped me a lot not to focus on the mountain of issues that I saw, and to remember that the longest journey always begins with one step.

What this all boils down to is a basic need for us to begin by taking what little trust we have and placing it in the hands of a second family. This family, through their collective efforts, can help us resolve the developmental gaps in our history, face the shortcomings of our own humanity, rebuild a healthy foundation of memories upon which to grow and recover our family within.

How Did I Get Into This Mess Anyway?

As children, healthy memories provide us with a firm foothold on our developmental future. As adults, these same memories provide us with a cushion for our sanity. The lack of healthy memories undermines our developmental growth as children, and as adults leaves us with nothing concrete to draw on when times get tough. So it is that during periods of conflict and stress the adult child/co-dependent falls backward in time and becomes, as the term suggests, an adult who is acting like a dependent child.

The unhealthy memories of an adult who grew up in a troubled family get in the way of our better judgment and cause the parent in us to abandon the inner child. And this brings us back to that bus full of our inner family members.

Imagine for a moment that you're driving down the highway in your VW bug with your family, returning home from the state fair. Suddenly you hear the sound of a horn blasting in your ear. You glance up into the rearview mirror and see the front end of a big old yellow school bus bearing down on you. Your adrenaline starts pumping, you look again, and this time — to your horror — you realize that a *kid* is driving the bus.

Have you got the picture?

What do you do first? Right. You look for a safe place to pull over and get the heck out of the way. The very idea of a child trying to pilot a two-and-a-half-ton bus down a highway in heavy traffic, moving at 60 or 70 miles per hour, is frightening. Yet, ridiculous as it seems, this is exactly how I picture the adult child/co-dependent who is experiencing an emotional tolerance break.

An emotional tolerance break is a regressive, age-inappropriate, over-reactive emotional or behavioral episode. It occurs when something happens to overload your emotional circuits. The dam breaks and out pours a lifetime of bad news.

The crisis hits. You scramble around inside yourself, frantically searching for some healthy memory of adult logic or parental direction to guide you, but the cupboards are bare. So you panic. And while your inner adult and parent are busy trying to get their thumbs out of each others' noses, the child in you jumps in the front seat of the bus and starts driving. (This is the essence of the term adult child: a person who is an adult by reason of physical age, but who is emotionally a child.)

Why did the child jump into the driver's seat? Because it is the only way he or she knows how to survive. The parent and adult on the bus don't seem to have the foggiest idea of how to deal with crisis. Most adult child/co-dependents have a Ph.D. in survival. This is good because it has allowed us to come as far as we have. But survival alone is not a justification for what we are doing to ourselves and others.

The survival memories of sheer willpower, tenacity and perseverance are helpful, but these skills are not necessarily prerequisites to any real growth or change. Merely knowing how to survive was not enough for me. I needed to learn how to separate my past from my present and take my reactive inner child out of the driver's seat.

I know one thing for sure: When the child in our spirit gets behind the wheel of our bus we become reactors rather than responders. A *reactor* acts without a sense of choice; a *responder* acts with a sense of choice.

Instead of behaving like healthy adults or parents who know what their choices and responsibilities are, we behave like children who do not know what their choices are and who feel like victims. Consequently, during times of conflict or stress, we end up operating from a position of weakness instead of from a position of strength.

Together our lack of healthy childhood memories and sense of choice gets in the way of our better judgment.

Acting out of these deficits, we end up developing a negative philosophy about life: "Life's a bitch and then you die . . . Life is a no-win situation . . . The buzzing fly always gets the swatter . . . The glass is half empty . . . You made your own bed, now lie on it . . . Nice guys finish last . . . The end justifies the means."

Operating out of this kind of pessimistic belief system only serves to deepen the schism between the members of our inner family. These negative philosophies act like a wall of hopelessness to reinforce the process of self-abandonment and lend credence to the logic of a victim, which says we only deserve second best.

It is not for lack of intelligence that we sell ourselves short. On the contrary, it is precisely because of our intelligence that we managed to get so screwed up in the first place! As I said earlier, I have never met a stupid adult child or co-dependent and I don't expect I ever will.

It's Not Over 'Til It's Over

Adult child/co-dependents naively tell themselves, "The past is past; what's over is done." They say, "It will never happen to me like it did to my folks. I'm not going to make the same mistakes they did or do to my children what they did to me."

Sound familiar?

Well, I told myself these things too. As it turned out, however, nothing could have been further from the truth. This is not to say that I went out and did everything exactly as my parents had done it, but I didn't really manage to do it any better. I realized I simply had been playing the same game by a different name. The end result was more similar than different from what my parents had done.

Now I understand what developmental experts mean when they say we are basically what we have been taught to be: kind if we have been taught how to be kind; honest if we've been taught to be honest; happy if we've been taught how to be happy; and so on. We are the sum total of our life experiences, and it takes more than poems, promises, prayers and willpower to rewrite the script.

Slowly but surely I have come to accept that those lacks that first divided me from my family were the same lacks that first divided me from myself. In the same way these lacks had stunted the growth of my nuclear family, they also stunted the growth of my inner family.

Children are by definition unable to differentiate themselves from their surroundings. Thus they are often victims of the erroneous scripts of their family. The end result of this blind adherence to the family script is that they never learn to question who they are apart from their family.

For example, if the script says that children are somehow responsible for their parents' abandonment, neglect or abuse of them, then they might learn to see themselves as people who do not deserve to be cared for. As adults they are drawn toward people, places and things that reinforce this script.

Let's pretend that you're the child living in a troubled family where there is a lot of fighting and one alcoholic parent. One night you're lying in your room listening to your parents arguing in the hallway just outside your door. Your mom, who is drunk, accuses your dad of being out with another woman. He comes back at her with what a lousy housekeeper and mother she is. Next you hear your mom say, "Maybe if I didn't have to spend my whole day trying to keep up with that little brat who's sleeping in the next room, the house wouldn't be such a mess and I wouldn't need to drink just to get through another day with him!" Then your father says to her, "Maybe we would have been better off if we never had a kid in the first place."

How do you think you might feel?

Would you be wondering if your parents really loved you?

Would you begin to think that maybe they did not want you?

Do you think you might blame yourself for their problems?

Or, worse yet, would you think of yourself as a bad person?

No doubt you would be doing all of the above. Children are not immune to the hideous abuses, tensions and emotional traumas of a troubled family. Nor is their spirit resilient enough to withstand the kinds of insults that are levied against them by their parents. Tenacious, persevering and resourceful, yes; but resilient, no.

I often think of resiliency this way. You get up out of your chair, walk outside, take hold of a sledgehammer and put a couple of nice big dents in the hood of your car. You go back into the house, have some lunch and when you're done, you go back outside and find that all the dents you put in the hood have disappeared.

Now that's what I call resilience!

Literally, resilient means returning to or resuming the original shape; capable of withstanding shock without permanent deformation or rupture. Resilience is not an accurate word to use when trying to describe the apparent adaptive qualities of a child's spirit.

As adult child/co-dependents most of us learned well how to cover up all the psycho-emotional cuts and bruises that we suffered in our troubled families. But like the Bondo that we use to cover up rust and fill the dents of an old junker, it only takes a year or so of hard driving and weather before the Bondo begins to fall away and expose the true condition of the car.

As children we learn to mix up and apply our own kind of co-dependent Bondo in an effort to cover up the dents in our spirit. However, like the old junker, the stresses and strains of everyday life take their toll and the co-dependent Bondo of emotional denial falls away to expose the wounds of our troubled past.

Even though we manage to repress and even forget at times the details of those experiences that wounded or scarred our spirit, the emotional memories remain with us. Dormant, disconnected and fragmented as many of our memories may be, they continue to live in our subconscious.

It would be nice to know where our feelings are coming from, but it is not always possible. We need to learn that *feelings are facts* in and of themselves. They are neither innately good or bad, they just are. It is not how we feel that causes problems, it is how we choose to deal with our feelings that gets us in trouble. Similarly it is not *what* we think that is the problem, but what we *do* with what we think.

Perhaps the most destructive thing we do to our thoughts and feelings is deny them. A wise old man once told me that thoughts and feelings that are denied are thoughts and feelings that will find a behavioral reply.

Unfortunately the denial of basic thoughts and feelings is a classic symptom of troubled families, including the one that exists inside of us. When, consciously or unconsciously, we incorporate the dysfunctional rules of a troubled family into the fabric of our inner lives, we will inevitably begin to behave as our family behaved. Our inner family is no different than any other system. Whatever thoughts or feelings a family system denies will come out in some behavioral reply. These implicit nonverbal forms of expression become a metaphorical language that speaks to — but never directly about — the thoughts and feelings that the family says are not okay. It is the parent, adult and child in our spirit who learn to cope with those things that they refuse to talk about openly.

For example, as children growing up in a troubled family we learn to use lots of indirect forms of behavioral expression, such as running away from home, disobeying our parents, getting into fights, pouting, getting into trouble with the law, skipping classes, using drugs, being sexually promiscuous, getting pregnant, dropping out of school, lying or — at the other extreme — being a perfect child.

As adults who deny thoughts and feelings, we also learn to communicate indirectly by having affairs, being sexually inappropriate, getting drunk, overeating, gambling, not paying our bills, working too much, nagging, being violent or by neglecting, abandoning and abusing our children.

These dysfunctional adult patterns of behavior can point back to many things, but in most cases they boil down to the fact that we do not think we are okay and we do not love ourselves. This is the great revelation that most adult child/co-dependents run into on the road to recovering their family within. It is one thing to believe that others do not think we are okay or do not love us, but it is quite another thing when we discover that we think and feel this way about ourselves. Like it or not, we are all stuck with ourselves for the duration. As is often said, "Wherever you go, there you are."

Putting aside the dysfunctional patterns of avoidance, denial and repression is the only sure way to recover our inner family members and heal the emotional wounds that divide them. Until we emancipate ourselves from the script of our troubled family we will continue to live out someone else's life. The individual who fails to confront the dysfunctional scripts of the past is destined to repeat them.

A Crime And A Rhyme

Show me a child who is made to feel wrong, and I'll show you a child whose shame will be strong.

Show me a child who is covered in shame, and I'll show you a child who's a pawn in the game.

Show me a child who never broke free, and I'll show you a spirit that's destined to be . . . the next generation unwilling to see.

From childhood victim to adult volunteer, the spirit of shame is shrouded in fear.

Confront it they would, if they were not so afraid, but lacking in trust, they have nothing to trade.

So onward they travel pretending to be the kind of adult the world wants to see.

Co-dependent in spirit, and adult children all, they promise to change — with their backs to the wall.

Their struggle without mirrors their struggle within, these children of trauma who wear adult skin.

Half-spirits divided and lost in the game, they dress in delusion to shield them from blame.

Still, hope lies in conflict, and one day they'll see the truth of their folly and courage to be.

Four Faces
Of Identity

Sooner or later we are all faced with the question of who we are. For some this happens at 18, for others at 25 or 30. Still others may reach middle age before this happens. And, of course, there are those who, out of some real or imagined fear, never ask, "Who am I?"

Erikson and other developmental theorists have found that the majority of us tend to fit into one of four basic *identity types*. Which type we are depends largely upon our degree of commitment and whether or not we arrive at our commitment through a process of questioning. In this chapter we will take a look at these different identity types: *clear, questioning, frozen and fragmented.*

Clear Identity

These are the statements of a person with a clear identity:

- I know who I am.
- I have clear commitments.

- I have been working through a period of exploration, doubt, and questioning in order to arrive at this point.
- I am comfortable with myself.

Now let's listen to a woman with a clear identity. Ellen is 45 years old, a single parent of two teenage daughters. She works as a graphic artist for a large advertising firm. For the past three years she has been intimately involved with a man named Mitchell, whom she met through a mutual friend. When asked to give a brief description of herself, her response was straightforward and relaxed.

> I am a fairly traditional person with traditional values. I enjoy the work I do and take a great deal of pride in the job I have done raising my two daughters. I can be a stubborn person at times, but for the most part I would say I am pretty easy-going. I am not an extrovert by any stretch of the imagination, and I much prefer the intimate company of a few close friends to a big cocktail party or a night on the town. I have a couple of really close friends whom I share myself with, but I also make sure to carve out time every week just for me.
>
> My daughters like me, although they regularly tease me about being too fussy about the house, which I know I am, and about being "boring," which by their standards I'm sure I am. I think that I am a warm and loving person, and Mitchell and I have a really good relationship. He has his own outside interests, which I appreciate, and he values the fact that I too have my own interests.

In describing her path to this stage in her life, Ellen speaks with more affect in her voice.

> I cannot believe how much I have changed! Ten years ago I was an emotional mess! Talk about a roller-coaster ride. I had gone straight from home into a marriage at the age of 20 and had two children before our third anniversary. John and I set out to live the American Dream. We bought a house. I was a full-time Mom, and he worked long hours. Everyone thought we were the perfect couple. Well, the best-laid plans often go awry. We were really just a couple of kids in adult bodies. Our immaturity and inability to let go of each other finally drove us apart.
>
> I started hopping from one short-term relationship to another. I used having sex as a way out of my loneliness and desperation. I made a lot of bad relationship choices during that period of my life. For a time I even got involved with a guy who physically abused me. Finally, as a result of that relation-

ship, I woke up to the insanity of what I was doing, got myself a job and sought out some much-needed professional guidance. With a lot of help from my counselor I was able to take a long hard look at myself and what I was doing. Thank God, I am still young enough to enjoy my life. I like myself now, and at 45 I can honestly say that I am happier than I have ever been. Best of all, I know who I am.

Questioning Identity

These are the statements of a person with a questioning identity:

- I am anxious and questioning.
- I am no longer satisfied with the way things are.
- I am actively seeking and systematically exploring.
- I am both excited and scared about the possibility of a new future.

Greg has a questioning identity. He is a 33-year-old executive vice president of research and development for a large toy manufacturing company. Talented and ambitious, Greg moved quickly up the corporate ladder. Along with his wife and three children, Greg lives in a beautiful home just outside of New York in a prestigious bedroom community. Work and family are at the center of Greg's life and he prides himself in what he has managed to accomplish. Greg grew up with an alcoholic mother and a workaholic father, who divorced while he was still in grade school. In response to the query "Who am I?" he gave the following response:

> After my parent's divorce my mother became increasingly dependent on me for emotional support. Because I was the oldest child my mother put me in the position of caretaker for the rest of my brothers and sisters. For a long time, well into my 20s, I took at lot of pride in being the "responsible" one in my family. Strange as it sounds, I was like a husband to my mom and like a father to all my siblings. I was one powerful guy, if you know what I mean.
>
> I didn't leave home until I was 25, got married at 29 and carried my be-all-and-do-all attitude right into my new life. My career took off like a shot, and I was on my way to what I thought was going to be a perfect life. Then, about a year ago, when I turned 33, things started to get shaky.
>
> I just didn't feel right inside. Little things started to bother me, and for the first time in my life I was having trouble

sleeping. I would wake up cranky and short-tempered. I would launch into my wife and kids for no reason. It got so bad that even the dog was afraid to be around me. This went on for several months until I began to have migraine headaches. My doctor told me that I had high blood pressure and put me on several different kinds of medication.

Unfortunately the drugs didn't do a thing for any of my other symptoms. I still couldn't sleep at night and I was certainly no less of an ogre. My family was really beginning to worry about me. I could not figure it out. Everything had been going so well. I was so sure of myself. Finally, going against my life-long belief that I could go it alone, I decided to seek out professional help. That was probably the hardest thing I have ever done — asking for help. I mean, it was a real blow to my ego.

Anyway, I've been in therapy now for about a year and my wife and kids have become involved recently too. The most important thing that has come out of this for me so far is that I needed to take some time to stop and look at myself, where I came from and where I was going. I had never done anything like that before. Now I am going to decide what it is that I "really" want to do when I grow up, how I "really" want to live my life and how I can emancipate myself from the co-dependent script of my childhood, the script of savior, protector, provider and "strong one."

I do not know how it will all turn out — my life, I mean. Most of the time I just feel scared and excited. I guess it is normal to feel this way. And while I am pretty uneasy about not having all the answers, it is a comforting thought to know I do not have to. Like my therapist always says, "The man who knows he's lost knows a lot."

Frozen Identity

The statements of a person with a frozen identity are:

- I *think* I know who I am.
- I *appear* to be happy and even prosperous.
- I do all the right things.
- I act as if I am okay even though at some level I am aware of being unhappy.
- I feel anxious and afraid beneath my outward calm.
- My life is not my own.

Carrie is 35, married to a successful attorney, the mother of two and a college graduate with a degree in art history. She is very attractive, well-liked in her community and has received several awards for her volunteer work. She is considered to be an excellent hostess, seems to get along wonderfully with her parents — who live in the same town — and is generally admired by everyone as being a pillar of the community.

To the question, "Who am I?" Carrie replies:

> I am a mother, a wife, a devoted daughter, hard-working community volunteer, scout leader, church volunteer . . . you know, I never realized how much I do during a typical day. How do I feel about my life?

She pauses for a long time.

> I have never said this to anyone, but lately I haven't been feeling right. At first I thought it was the flu, or that I was just tired from overwork. But there's something else. I have been anxious for no apparent reason. And I have been feeling so mechanical — sort of numb, just going through the motions. I feel terrible even saying this! I just keep thinking, "How many women would give their eye teeth to be where I am right now?" Something is wrong. Something is happening. I cannot believe this. I feel trapped. I have it all and I feel trapped with nowhere to go.

Tears begin to well up in her eyes.

> Yesterday, for the first time in my life, I really felt angry toward my parents. It is just not right. They've given me everything. Why do I feel this way?

Carrie regains her composure and relaxes a little.

> It's probably just my PMS acting up again. I forgot what time of the month it was. I really should get back in to see my doctor about this. Of course, I'll be fine after I have my period. I always feel more like myself after that . . . really, I do.

Fragmented Identity

The statements of a person with a fragmented identity are:

- I do not know who I am.
- I may have known who I am.
- I flit from one idea to the next, from one relationship to the next.

- I am not systematically seeking or exploring.
- I am in constant motion in order to stay out of touch with myself.
- Beneath it all I feel anxious, lost and confused.

Mike is a 24-year-old college senior who works part-time on weekends as a waiter in a local restaurant. After high school he worked for a year, then went to a junior college, then worked for another year before attending the university where he is graduating with a low C average in business administration. He is very attractive, charming and at first appears to be solid and confident. When asked, "Who am I?" he replies,

> You know, that's a good question. My father has been asking me that for years.

He smiles and laughs.

> No, seriously though, I see myself as pretty much of a free spirit. You know, I am responsible, going to college and all, but my friends see me as the life of the party. They know how smart I am with women, too. I always keep my options open. Nobody's going to pin me down! If things start getting too close, I just kiss 'em goodbye and go with the next one. Parties? Yeah, pretty much every weekend. I get smashed Saturday night for sure, and sometimes we'll start Friday afternoon and end late Sunday night.

He laughs.

> Boy, I'm glad I don't have any early morning classes on Mondays.

Mike laughs again. When asked about his goals for the next five years, Mike answers,

> Goals? Well, I don't know. I'm having too much fun right now to worry about goals. I'll probably get into some kind of management training program or something like that. I don't want anything too demanding where there's a lot of responsibility or routine. You know, my lifestyle is the greatest! We wouldn't want to tamper with that, right? Marriage? Naw. Women are certainly lots of fun, if you know what I mean . . . but the same one for 20 or 30 years? No way! I need my freedom. Variety is the spice of life.

What Is Identity Development?

It is extremely important to keep a few points in mind as we explore these four identity types. First and foremost, identity development has no rigid parameters. It is an ongoing process of working through and refining our understanding of who we are. For example, it would not be unusual for someone to have found a clear sense of identity and then be thrown into yet another identity crisis by the death of a spouse or a debilitating illness.

The main thing to remember is that our identity is not etched in stone and that we have the ability to learn from our mistakes. The individual who has successfully faced and worked through identity issues in the past will have more of the tools necessary to work through future ones.

Second, it is possible to be clear in one area of identity and frozen in another. For example, a person may have found his or her vocational calling through a process of questioning, but still be stuck with respect to relationships of political or spiritual beliefs.

Third, there is always a danger in using labels or stereotypes when it comes to identity. Too often they are misused or wind up sounding like an indictment. For example, Sally says to her spouse, "See? According to this book you're stuck and I'm not. I've already been through my crisis period, so I must be what they refer to here as a clear identity. I would think you're getting tired of chasing your tail. Lord knows, I am. Why don't you do something?"

Having a clear identity means that one is comfortable deep inside. It precludes the need to judge others. Sally's comments are a common example of how labels get abused.

Fourth, research shows that the longer we remain frozen in our identity, the harder it may be to get into a questioning state that would lead to a clear identity. In short, it is hard to teach an old dog new tricks.

Fifth, and perhaps most confusing, is the fact that people who enter into a state of questioning around midlife are often accused of being fragmented, immature or emotionally dysfunctional when the truth is that they might be healthier than they have ever been. Sometimes it is difficult to distinguish between the questioning and fragmented identity states. By the same token, people who seem to have a clear identity state may actually be frozen. The lesson in all this is an old one: Never judge a book by its cover.

The Shame
Of It All

Coming to grips with the issue of co-dependency in my own life was a rather confusing revelation that threw my identity into a state of total confusion. From the moment I first began to think of myself as a "double winner" — alcoholic and co-dependent — everything seemed to change. It was as if someone had turned on a bright light in a dark room. And that room was filled with every kind of emotional memory.

I saw memories of my mother's drinking. Memories of my drinking. Memories of being small and listening to my parents fight. Scary memories of long nights and anxious moments. Memories of my sisters crying and of me crying. Childish memories built on lofty dreams and great expectations. Fractured memories of spoiled holidays, missed moments and broken promises. Bittersweet memories that caused my stomach to churn.

Flashbacks to long summers, youthful adventures, old friends, my dog Spunky, playing in a rock band, falling out of my crib and breaking my collar bone, driving to California, hunting with my dad, skipping school, hating myself, feeling stupid, discovering girls, acting strong, feeling weak, being afraid, getting drunk, being arrested, going to military school, flunking out, feeling retarded, watching friends go off to war, going to college, feeling like a phoney, drinking to feel normal, worrying about how others saw me, smashing up my car, getting sober, becoming a Christian, getting married, having a child, getting divorced, being angry, losing my job, lying to myself and playing the fool.

This avalanche of memories and emotions left me wondering which end was up. My identity was in a major state of transition.

Where once there had been clarity, there was now only confusion, and where once there had been confidence, there was now only uncertainty.

My thoughts were a jumble. *"Maybe I have finally gone off the deep end. I am having a nervous breakdown or maybe I am on a dry drunk. No, I'm having a midlife crisis. Yeah, that's it, I'm having a midlife crisis, But wait — I can't be having a midlife crisis, I'm only 29. What in God's name is wrong with me?"*

I was at war with myself emotionally and didn't know why.

I had been kidnapped by my past and placed on trial for every mistake I had ever made and every debt I hadn't paid. The list of charges against me seemed endless. It felt like an indictment of my whole life. When it was finally over and the verdict had come in, I had found myself guilty on all counts: guilty as a child, guilty as a son, guilty as a friend, guilty as a father and worst of all, guilty as a person.

There I was, trapped inside myself, wishing that I had never been born. More than a verdict of guilt, however, the judgment I had levied against myself was one of shame. I knew I had made my share of mistakes growing up, but nothing that would have warranted such harsh treatment. Innocent as my inner child may have been, there was no escaping the hostile pursuit of my guilting inner adult and my shaming inner parent.

Finally, exhausted from the ordeal, I reluctantly decided to take the advice of an old AA friend and just let go. He assured me that my Higher Power would take care of it and that in good time an answer would come. As usual, he was right. When the clouds did part, the answer I got was almost too simple for me to accept.

The answer? I didn't like myself.

It seems clear to me now that the denial of my past had been a denial of my feelings, and that the denial of my feelings had been tantamount to a denial and abandonment of myself as a person. The collective message was that I was no better than my history and my history was wrong.

Unwittingly I had fallen victim to the mistaken logic of a child: I had taken on the shame of my family as my own.

> *THE WEDGE OF SHAME:* The private logic that says there is something wrong with us is the wedge of shame that ultimately divides us from ourselves and others.

A Wall Of Shame

Inside the void I stood alone and questioned not the solemn tone.

The voices spoke in anger clear, but never lent a loving ear.

It must be me, the thought occurred, the judgment made, the pictures blurred.

"That's right, it's me," a voice did say, "and mark my words, one day you'll pay."

Then hide I will behind this wall, its mortar strong and structure tall.

And in this place I know I'll find the time to heal and solve the crime.

Yet nothing changed from year to year because I chose to live in fear.

How wrong I was to build this frame that locked out love and nurtured shame.

For the child of my youth, you see, was innocent but never free.

And through the lonely days that passed, I came to know the truth at last.

No fault should I have placed on he, who worked so hard to rescue me.

Now on the road behind I see the emptiness that followed me.

Through wisdom gained across the years, I've finally learned to face my fears.

United now, with child in hand, I've staked my claim and made my stand.

That wall of shame that once I knew has been replaced with love that's true.

And now I'm whole, no longer bound, forgiven all and freedom found.

The Tragic Legacy Of Unresolved Anger

"Cunning, powerful and baffling" were the terms first used by Alcoholics Anonymous to describe the insidious nature of alcoholism. I use these same terms today to describe the insidious nature of co-dependency.

For the first six years of my recovery from alcoholism I was out of touch with the significance of my adult child history. As my recovery progressed, however, I came to recognize that the cunning, baffling and powerful dimensions of my alcoholism were little more than the subtle reflections of my unresolved co-dependency.

The realization of my own co-dependency was by no means a small event. For the first time in my life I had actually begun to face the emotional reality of my past. The floodgates opened and every sort of feeling rushed forth. I felt like a man running the gauntlet. I was out of control and with every passing wave of emotion I felt more and more ashamed.

"Why is this happening to me?" I asked. Nothing could have felt more wrong to me. I had always taken pride in my ability to rise above my feelings. But somehow I'd been stripped of my honor, banished from the company of real men and reduced to a wimp. How could I have let these emotional phantoms get the best of me?

Take my anger, for example, an emotion that my father had absolutely no time for. Never during my growing-up years did I ever hear my father say that he was angry about anything. What I do remember, though, was how ashamed I felt whenever I got angry in front of my dad and he'd give me one of those disapproving looks he was so good at. Just thinking about those times made me angry. After all, my mother's alcoholism and my father's co-dependency had taken an emotional toll on me that I had never dealt with and had been storing up for the past 25 years. Small wonder that everyone who knew me thought of me as an angry man.

Then it finally came to me: "I'm an angry man."

I had never admitted this to myself before, but the shoe fit. The mere thought brought back memories of all the times I had lost my temper or taken my anger out on someone. Even as a sober man my interactions with people were very often hostile and aggressive. Fast forward or full reverse were the only two choices I knew back then. I began to realize just how much of my life had been controlled by anger over the unfinished business of my past.

Not all kids survive or overcome the emotional traumas of having grown up in a troubled family system. Tragically the cumulative layers of emotional denial, rejection and abandonment can lead to a premature end. I learned those lessons firsthand as a therapist several years ago when one of my young clients hung himself in the basement of his home. Despite all the warning signs — falling grades, isolation, anger and depression — his parents were unable to see past their own problems long enough to recognize what his behavior was saying to them. When he tried to talk to them directly, they would guilt and shame him for acting so wrapped up in himself. Even my professional warnings were not taken seriously.

This child's suicide touched me deeply and inspired me to write the following lines:

Children Of The Alcoholic

Dedicated To Chris S.

Compensators, controllers, manipulators, avoiders, deniers . . . all these and more are the many descriptive terms used to identify us. We are emotionally immature. We operate out of a framework filled with free-floating anxiety and fear as a result of the accumulated layers of unfinished business in our family history. We are most often motivated by guilt and shame, seeking always to relieve the internal stress of these emotional phantoms. We are spiritually divided from ourselves and unable to reveal to others what we ourselves can no longer see. Intimacy is a goal. But as individuals not familiar or intimate with ourselves, we are unable to develop real closeness with another. Lost, defiant, confused, pessimistic, mistrusting, angry and afraid, we have become defensive and seek only from those who are like us.

Black and white are the attitudes we hide behind so as to avoid the stressful feelings that always precede change. Crying for help in a language that few understand, wishing to be heard but denying the confrontations of truth . . . liars who have the truth but believe, as the wounded child in our history, that we will as before be hurt in our sharing. Running, always running, creating the crisis only to divert the pain and hide in the clouds of confusion. We have survived by our wits and our will. We must not be broken but shaped by the constancy of love that holds firmly to those values which promote life, model wholeness and give hope. Only these things will we hear, for the child in us believes as a victim and sees no choice or avenue of escape.

Breaking free of co-dependency is not easy, but it is possible. It is your choice. Getting to know the members of your inner family will help you to be able to make that choice. In the next section we'll take a close look at the parent, adult and child within each and every one of us.

PART THREE

Discovering The Family Within

For adult children the denial of honest emotion begins at a very young age and eventually leads to a profound division of spirit. It is this division of spirit that sparks the development of a defensive, co-dependent pattern of coping.

These outward patterns of co-dependency are little more than the symptoms of our fragmented inner family.

> *A Spirit Divided: The adult child/co-dependent is a spirit divided from itself. Recovery requires a balanced integration of the inner parent, the inner adult and the inner child.*

As I began to understand my own co-dependency, it became increasingly apparent to me that how I portrayed myself on the outside was inconsistent with how I was thinking or feeling on the inside. My ability to put on a false front was only part of a sophisticated game that I had learned as a child in an effort to disguise my underlying feelings of self-doubt and shame. The logic of my co-dependency was deeply rooted in the mind of a frightened child who lived in my spirit and believed that he was not okay.

In this section we will take a long look at the structure of our inner family — who they are, how they communicate and how we can begin to heal them.

Dimensions Of
The Spirit

The concept of an inner parent, an inner adult and an inner child is by no means a new idea. It was first introduced by Eric Berne in a theory he called Transactional Analysis or TA.

A Brief Look At TA

According to Berne the intrapersonal spirit is made up of a three-dimensional matrix consisting of an inner parent, adult and child. Berne's postulations of parent, adult and child do correspond to Freudian theories of superego, ego and id, although the two theories should not be confused. As Berne suggests: "The cordial relationship between psychoanalysis [Freudian theory] as core and Transactional Analysis as the apple indicates that the core fits more readily within the apple than vice versa."

When we describe interpersonal communications using a TA model we make two basic assumptions. First, healthy interaction or communication between two or more adults is possible only as long as the transactional process remains parallel — that is, each party is operating as an adult and communicating out of an adult ego. Second, if there is a crossing of the transactional vectors (ego states) in the interaction, then an unhealthy or inappropriate communication between individuals results. The figures 11.2 and 11.3 illustrate these two points.

Instead of direct lines of communication between the two adult ego states, as indicated by arrow 1, party A is operating out of his/her inner child and party B is operating out of his/her inner parent as indicated by arrow 2. This kind of transaction would only be appropriate if party A were in fact a child and party B were in fact his/her parent.

A healthy and productive transaction between two or more adults means that each must be operating consistently out of an adult ego state. This does not mean, however, that the remaining ego states of parent and child in each party are not important to the organization and eventual delivery of a healthy interpersonal adult transaction. It simply means that they are not the appropriate agents through which adults should be trying to communicate or interact with one another. TA clearly assumes that the only way to build and maintain a close, trusting, autonomous and lasting intimate relationship between two adults is through a process of adult transactional parallelism or, as outlined in Figure 11.3, adult to adult.

In Figure 11.2 there is no parallelism, and the result is crossed communications. The consequence of these crossed transactional vectors is that the parties are not relating to one another as adult equals or mature partners.

To illustrate this very important point further, let's say that adult B, who is operating out of the inner adult, begins a transactional sequence with adult A by saying,

"You look as if there's something bothering you."

Angrily A comes back with, "No one cares about me and nobody ever will."

Hooked emotionally by the childish message of adult A, adult B reacts as a parent instead of remaining an adult and says, "Why, that's just not true. I'm a somebody and I care about you."

Stuck in the inner child, person A looks at person B and blurts out, "No you don't. You're only saying that to try to cover up your real feelings about me."

Still unaware of adult A's manipulative maneuvering, adult B continues to be unconsciously hooked into the role of parent and says,

"No, I'm not trying to cover anything up. I really care about you and I always will."

Need I go on? The obvious lack of mutuality, balance and transactional parallelism in this example demonstrates how easily the lines of adult interpersonal communication can become crossed. Instead of two adults relating to one another in a healthy fashion, you get one acting out the role of a child and the other acting out the role of a parent (see Figure 11.4).

This is neither a healthy nor productive style of adult communication. At best it is a perfect example of how *not* to do things.

Such breakdowns in communication are common among adult child/co-dependents primarily because they lack a clear understanding of their own intrapersonal family. This lack of internal clarity is often the product of having lived in a dysfunctional system where the roles of parent, adult and child were poorly modeled. Unfortunately for these children the modeling of unhealthy ego states by parents and other adult caregivers become the unhealthy prototypes for their own intrapersonal family. The interpersonal failings of the parents become the intrapersonal shortcomings of the child. Inevitably such children grow up to be adults who fail at close relationships with others because they fail to have a healthy relationship with themselves. Because the intrapersonal relationship needs to come first, our focus from now on will be on the how-tos of healing the family within.

Communication Styles Of The Family Within

The formation of a clear adult identity depends on many factors, not the least of which is the formation of a healthy intrapersonal relationship. From a TA perspective this means developing a healthy relationship between the parent, adult and child dimensions of our ego. This is not an easy thing for most adult children/co-dependents to do. Why? Because in addition to their problems with things like trust, autonomy, initiative and industry, they carry with them a distorted perspective of what being a healthy parent, adult and child is really all about.

Certainly this was true in my case. It wasn't until I became acquainted with the concept of TA that I began to see just how distorted and out of sync I really was with myself. I saw in Berne's ordering of the inner parent, adult and child ego states a prophetic picture. Instead of a benign developmental structure, as intended by Berne, I saw his alignment of the intrapersonal family as a perfect example of a co-dependent system. This system was hierarchical in design and placed the child in a subordinate position. It was also a divisive system, in which the parent-child relationship was nonexistent. Finally, it was a linear system that allowed no open interaction or direct communication between all three parts of the ego.

From a systems perspective, the only functional alternative to this model would be one where all three parts are given equal status. Figure 11.6 is an illustration of how I believe this could be accomplished.

Reorganizing the structure of the inner family in this new way accomplishes several important objectives. First and foremost, it brings together the inner parent and child. Second, it removes the adult as go-between for the parent and the child. Third, it creates a truly interactive system.

Assuming that the hierarchical model of the intrapersonal family (Figure 11.5) is, in fact, a co-dependent model, then recovery from the dis-ease of co-dependency means completely restructuring the family within. In this respect I see the circular ordering (Figure 11.6) of the inner family as the only workable alternative. Figure 11.7 graphically illustrates the structural and operational differences between these two models.

Discovering The Nature Of Co-Dependency

Needless to say, you can't change what you can't see. But thanks to the work of people like Erik Erikson, Eric Berne, Virginia Satir and Bill Wilson, we have arrived at a time when we can actually define the structure of our intrapersonal lives. Child development, TA, systems theory and the primary disease concept all provide clues to the nature of co-dependency and its relationship to our family within. Therefore I believe it is extremely important for the recovering individual to have at least a working knowledge of these theories. To this end, let's take a moment to review these four theories:

1. *Child development:* This theory teaches us that there are specific stages in our psycho-emotional growth and that our ability to be intimate with ourselves and others depends on the successful resolution of these stages. The outward symptoms of co-dependency are a reflection of a delayed intrapersonal identity.

2. *Family systems theory:* The system model teaches that we are more than just a product of genetics and that our

social, cultural, extended and nuclear families all play a part in shaping our personality. Systems theory also teaches us that the rules of the family set the stage for the development of coping patterns on both the interpersonal and intrapersonal levels.

3. *Transactional Analysis:* TA provides us with a three-dimensional model of our ego that, when combined with the principles of systems theory, can be used to define the functional versus the dysfunctional organizational structure of our intrapersonal family. "Functional," in this case, refers to the circular organization of the family within and "dysfunctional" refers to the linear or hierarchical organization.

4. *Primary disease concept:* This concept teaches us that a chemically dependent or otherwise compulsively addicted individual who wants to recover must first achieve a state of sobriety and/or abstinence from the primary addiction. Although there are always exceptions to the rule, this is generally a safe axiom to follow.

Each of these theories relates to a different aspect of the adult child/co-dependent struggle and lends credence to the idea of an inner family whose very identity and well-being depend upon the formation of a trusting relationship between its members. Central to this goal is the development of healthy values that are supported by the rules of the system. If the rules of the system do not support the values, the result is a conflicted relationship between the inner parent, adult and child.

For example, if we believe that honesty is always the best policy, but the rules say, "It's not okay to share negative thoughts or feelings" or "It's wrong to say anything that might upset the status quo," then instead of being true to our values we end up compromising them. This "Do as I say, not as I do" behavior is precisely the kind of thing that stunts our developmental growth, divides our spirit and leads us into a self-destructive, co-dependent lifestyle.

So it is through a blending of basic principles borrowed from child development, family systems theory, TA and the primary disease concept that I have come to define co-dependency as a delayed identity development syndrome of the family within. It is an emotional, psychological and behavioral pattern of coping brought on by a prolonged exposure to and practice of a set of dysfunctional rules.

Who Are Members Of The Family Within?

Now that we have discovered that we have a family within our spirit, the next step in recovery is to work on defining the who's who of our intrapersonal family. This may be confusing at the start, but rest assured that the confusion is normal and only temporary.

The first thing to do is sit down and put together a list of terms that you associate with being a parent, an adult and a child. Include both the positive as well as the negative characteristics and don't be afraid to draw on your own experience. The purpose of this exercise is simply to try and establish a balanced profile for each dimension of our intrapersonal family. A single paragraph of descriptive adjectives on each member of the family is all that is required. Here's an example of how these profiles might look:

1. Parent: Nurturing, shaming, abusive, supportive, rigid, caring, judgmental, patient, punishing, loving, neglectful, protective, critical, strong, weak, respectful, rejecting, unconditional, intrusive, trustworthy, conditional, moral, condescending, ethical, impatient, giving, untrustworthy, warm, cold, steady, overbearing, committed, consoling, controlling and *powerful.*

2. Adult: Intellectual, logical, rational, analytical, nonemotional, guilting, factual, calculating, cold, intentional, purposeful, delusional, amoral, cognitive, deliberate and *cunning.*

3. Child: Loving, dishonest, open, stubborn, giving, needy, playful, emotional, impulsive, affective, greedy, vulnerable, tenacious, manipulative, instinctive, lustful, intuitive, defiant, honest, spontaneous, dependent, narcissistic, persevering, adaptive, self-centered, obstinate, creative, reluctant, trusting, reactive, unpredictable and *baffling.*

As you may have gathered, a number of characteristics are shared by all three members of the family. These traits sometimes make it difficult to distinguish one from the other. In general terms, however, the roles are defined as follows:

1. The *parent* is the protective, nurturing and moral guide of the system.
2. The *adult* is the rational, logical and intellectual guide of the system.
3. The *child* is the emotional, intuitive and creative guide of the system.

It is very important to remember that *only parent and adult characteristics can be given a positive or negative value.* The characteristics of a child's profile are neither good nor bad, they just are. In short, a child can't help being a child — which cannot be said about the role of parent or adult. Parents and adults may be ignorant or unaware of their choices, but they are never free from the responsibility of their choices. For them, ignorance of the law is no excuse.

The child in our spirit is innocent. He or she is capable of wrong thinking, erroneous beliefs, emotional distortions, inappropriate desires and selfish obsession, but innocent nevertheless. Only the parent and adult can be considered responsible agents in our family within. We must make these important adjustments in our thinking if we are ever to move beyond the legacy of a co-dependent past.

Relieving the child within from the burden of having to be more than a child is the first critical step in healing the family within. Clearly, if the goal in recovery is to establish a sense of "well-being," then it seems obvious that we must come to a nonjudgmental perspective of our inner child and his or her role in the family. If we continue to think of him or her as a warped or deviant member of the family, it will be impossible for us ever to trust in the emotional and intuitive wisdom that comes to us through the child.

It is up to our inner parent and adult to unravel the distorted emotional logic and dysfunctional rules that divide our family within. It is not the child in our spirit who needs rehabilitating, it is the parent and adult. They alone possess the intellectual and moral competence to face the real world. What the child in our spirit needs most is for our inner parent and adult to get their acts together.

The biggest obstacle in the path of our child's recovery is the continued verbal, emotional and psychological abuse, neglect and abandonment of our co-dependent inner parent and adult.

So: *Who* is it in you who needs treatment in order to recover? I hope you see that it is your inner adult and parent.

Mapping Out Your Family Within

One way to get to know the members of your inner family is to draw a map showing their relative size and importance.

Consider the case of Tom, who grew up in a family where it was not okay for him to show his feelings. His parents were strict disciplinarians who believed that children should be seen and not heard and that to spare the rod was to spoil the child. According to Tom his mother was a religious junkie who spent the majority of her time reading the Bible and preaching to him about the evils of the flesh. His father, on the other hand, was a true stoic. He believed that "real" men are above emotion, free of passion, unmoved by joy or grief and totally indifferent to pain and suffering. Tom said his dad was a man with ice in his veins.

As a result of his upbringing Tom was in a constant state of emotional turmoil, and in the beginning of treatment he didn't know a thought from a feeling. Gradually, however, the fog lifted and Tom began to see how the dysfunctional rules of his family had stunted his emotional growth. It was at this point that Tom began to recognize the existence of his inner family.

For the next month I worked with Tom on sorting out the three dimensions of his inner family and defining each of their roles. Once this task had been accomplished, I had Tom draw up a map of his inner family, using circles to describe the relative size and position of each member. Tom put together the following illustration of his family within (see Figure 11.8).

A picture is worth a thousand words; and for Tom, as for most adult child/co-dependents, seeing is believing. In Tom's case seeing the obvious disparity between his inner parent, adult and child made it clear that it was not his child who was at fault, but his parent and adult who were at the root of his problem. Armed with this new understanding Tom was able to break through the remaining clouds of emotional confusion and enter into a more proactive role in his own recovery.

Once he had uncovered the cause of his problem, the next step was to develop a strategy for change. First, Tom put a moratorium on the shilting (guilting and shaming) behaviors of his inner parent and adult. Next, he made a concerted effort to reaffirm the inner child and make amends to him by correcting the abusive patterns of his inner parent and adult. The final and most difficult step in Tom's recovery plan was to heal the broken bonds of trust between the three dimensions of his inner spirit and teach them to work together as a unit.

The further along Tom got in his recovery process, the more he understood how his inner parent and adult had abandoned and rejected his inner child. Tom's journey was far from over. But, based on this insight, he was able to bring about some major changes in the organizational structure of his inner family (see Figure 11.9).

Tom's maps of his inner family are fairly typical of how things look inside the spirit of a practicing adult child/co-dependent, but they represent only two possible variations on the theme. The disease of co-dependency has many faces, and to my way of thinking the exercise of mapping out the inner family is an excellent way to put a face to a name. This approach provides us with a visual image of how the inner parent, adult and child relate to one another. To put it simply, "What we can name, we can tame."

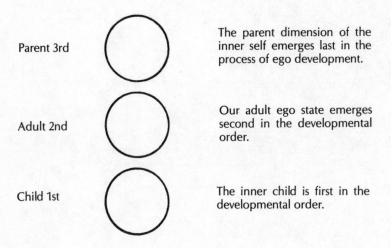

Parent 3rd — The parent dimension of the inner self emerges last in the process of ego development.

Adult 2nd — Our adult ego state emerges second in the developmental order.

Child 1st — The inner child is first in the developmental order.

Figure 11.1. The TA Model Of Ego Development

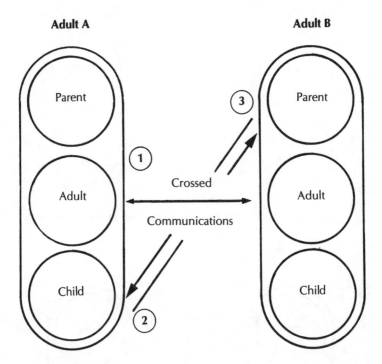

Instead of direct lines of communication between the two adult ego states as indicated by Arrow 1, party A is operating out of his/her inner child as indicated by Arrow 2 and party B is operating out of his/her inner parent as indicated by Arrow 3. This kind of transaction would only be appropriate if party A were in fact a child and party B were in fact his/her parent.

Figure 11.2. Unhealthy Crossed Communication Between Adults

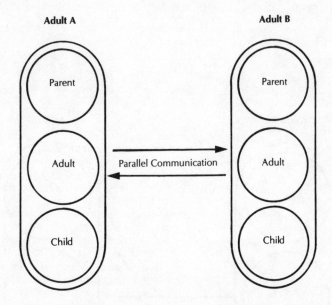

Figure 11.3. Healthy Parallel Communication Between Adults

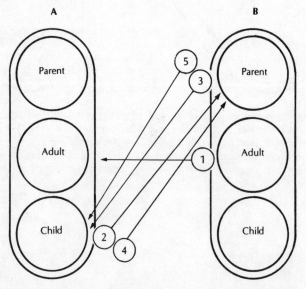

Figure 11.4. Co-dependent Transaction Between Two Adults

1. This is a *hierarchical* model. The child is a third-class citizen within the family structure. Visually it appears as though the child in this family has been given a room in the cellar of the house. Anyway you look at it, the child comes in last.

Co-dependent Model

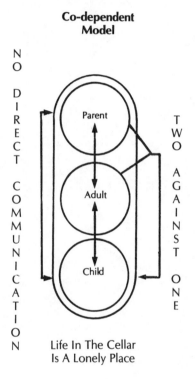

N O D I R E C T   C O M M U N I C A T I O N

T W O   A G A I N S T   O N E

Life In The Cellar
Is A Lonely Place

2. In this co-dependent model of the inner family the adult is always standing between the parent and the child, preventing any direct communication. Since the child will never learn to trust the parent, he/she is forced to look outside the inner family for validation, acceptance, nurturing and love. What parental support there is must always be channeled to the child through the adult. Because of this "contaminated parenting," the child never feels okay.

3. This hierarchical model is a rigid structure that does not allow for the open exchange of information between the inner parent, adult and child.

Figure 11.5. Model Of The Co-dependent Family Within

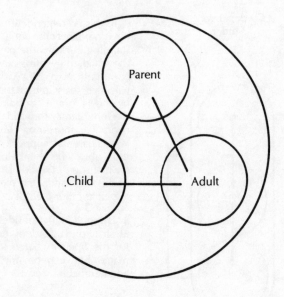

Figure 11.6. Model Of The Healthy Family Within

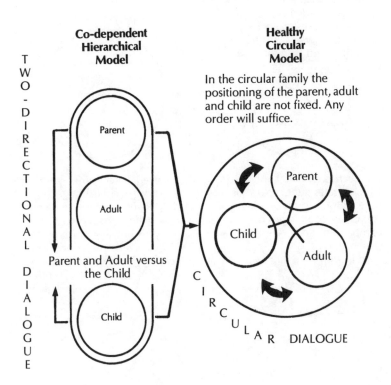

Figure 11.7. Comparison Between Original And Adapted TA
Models: Linear And Circular Communication

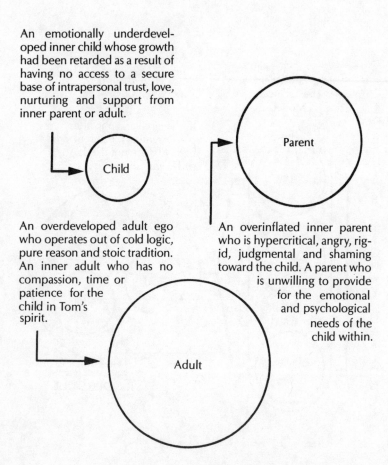

An emotionally underdeveloped inner child whose growth had been retarded as a result of having no access to a secure base of intrapersonal trust, love, nurturing and support from inner parent or adult.

An overdeveloped adult ego who operates out of cold logic, pure reason and stoic tradition. An inner adult who has no compassion, time or patience for the child in Tom's spirit.

An overinflated inner parent who is hypercritical, angry, rigid, judgmental and shaming toward the child. A parent who is unwilling to provide for the emotional and psychological needs of the child within.

Figure 11.8. Tom's Map Of His Inner Family After One Month Of Recovery

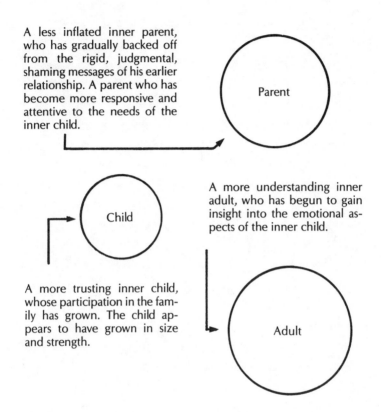

A less inflated inner parent, who has gradually backed off from the rigid, judgmental, shaming messages of his earlier relationship. A parent who has become more responsive and attentive to the needs of the inner child.

Parent

A more understanding inner adult, who has begun to gain insight into the emotional aspects of the inner child.

Child

A more trusting inner child, whose participation in the family has grown. The child appears to have grown in size and strength.

Adult

Figure 11.9. Tom's Map Of His Inner Family After One Year Of Recovery

Suicide, Murder
And Maim

Suicide

Have you ever thought about committing suicide? I must admit there were times in my life when I considered it. I'm glad I chose life instead. What fascinates me now about those suicidal episodes is not the reason why I wanted to end it all, but the reasons why I didn't. In hindsight I came up with a paradoxical understanding that the very things that made me want to kill myself were the same things that kept me from it.

For example, the main reasons I felt like exiting stage left was my overwhelming sense of guilt and shame. But my thoughts of suicide made me feel so "shilty" that I couldn't have done it. Crazy as it sounds, I have to thank my flaming co-dependent inner parent and adult for saving my life. If it had not been for their guilting and shaming ways, I don't think I would have made it to my thirtieth birthday.

If ever they had done me a favor, it was then — and what a formidable psycho-emotional tag team they were. Without much effort I can still recall the sounds of their voices as they ganged up on my suicidal inner child and shilted him out of killing himself. It went something like this . . .

Child: I don't deserve to live. I'm just a piece of dung. My life is a joke. I can't stand being me. What's the sense of going on? I think the world would be better off if I weren't here. Everything I do, everything I touch turns to poop. I'm going to kill myself and put an end to all my problems.

Adult: Now, that's the sickest thing I have ever heard. What are you, nuts? Only a crazy person, a wimp or a coward would think of taking the easy way out. I always knew you had a yellow streak running down your back. Real men don't run away from their responsibilities.

Parent: That's absolutely right. You should be ashamed of yourself for even thinking such a thing. No one in the Subby family has ever committed suicide and there is no way I'm going to allow you to soil our good name. Besides that, it goes against our religion. Do you really think that God would let you into heaven after taking your own life? No, I should say not. If I were you, I'd get my butt into church and pray to God to forgive me. Come to think of it, though, God probably wouldn't have the time of day for a wretch like you. Lord knows I wouldn't.

Adult: That's right. God has better things to do than sit around listening to people who can't even see past their own nose. Think about it, Bob. You're the guilty party here. You made your own bed and now you have to lie on it. So knock off all this "feeling" crap and pull yourself up by the bootstraps. That's what a healthy man would do in your place.

Parent: So, how do you want to be remembered, Bob — as the son who brought shame to his family or the son who made his family proud?

Finally after several rounds of relentless shilting and psychological abuse from the dynamic duo, my child withdrew his suicidal threat and retreated back into his shell to rethink his position. Being the manipulative, tenacious and creative street-fighter that he is, it wasn't long before he surfaced with a whole new strategy for coping with his pain.

Murder

Have you ever thought about committing murder? Come on now, be honest — you never *once* thought about how the death of a soon-to-be ex-spouse, sick parent, spiteful boss or some other wart on the face of humanity might not have been an easy solution to all your co-dependent problems?

There's nothing wrong with having had the thought. I know I did, and in all my travels I have yet to meet an adult child/co-dependent who hasn't. If you happen to be an exception to this rule, my apologies. At any rate, the idea of murder was destined to become another one of my inner child's misguided thoughts. I guess he must have figured that if he couldn't resolve his internal conflicts by taking his own life, then perhaps the answer would be to take someone else's.

Again, the guilt and shame that saved me from suicide were the same feelings that saved me from murder. The shilting tag-team of my inner parent and adult had done it again — and, of course, they were no less merciful or understanding than the time before.

Child: I know what my problem is now. It's not me, it's that boss of mine. He's out to get me and there are no two ways about it. I'm just going to have kill him and then I'll be okay.

Adult: Kill him! Is that what you said? I thought you were past all that sick thinking. Why if anyone else could hear what you're saying, they'd lock you in an institution for the criminally insane and throw away the key. Whatever hope I may have had for you is gone. You're a lost cause. One of the sickest people to ever walk on the planet.

Parent: Dear Lord have mercy on this child and purge him of these evil thoughts.

Adult: No amount of praying is going to help this boy. He's long past being helped.

Parent: Bob, can't you see what you're doing to us with all your blatant disrespect for God's laws? I don't have to remind you that murder is one of the big 10. Worse yet, you know that to have thought it is to have done it. In God's name, Bob, what is it you expect from us? Have you no shame?

Adult: I quit! You're a hopeless case, Bob.

As you can tell from this conversation, it was another no-win situation for my child.

Maim

My child recognized that there was only one last option open to him, an option that prompts me to ask you . . . *Have you stopped short of suicide or murder only to entertain the idea of "maim?"*

You know maim — as in withholding love, giving someone the silent treatment or being sarcastic. Most of us have done it at one time or another, and I became a master of maim. My child got so good at it that even he didn't know when he was doing it.

The "maim game" was the final strategy in my child's effort to cope with the pain of living inside a co-dependent family system. It was not a strategy of choice, but a strategy of necessity.

Maim, for the purposes of this discussion, refers to any act that causes injury or harm to one's psychological and emotional well-being. It is much more subtle than suicide or murder. The whole idea behind the maim game is to inflict pain without leaving any visible signs. The most widely practiced form of covert maiming is what the helping professions have long referred to as "passive aggression." So prevalent is this form of the maim game that it has earned its own place in the diagnostic manuals. To illustrate this particular aspect of the maim game I submit to you the following . . .

Maiming With Jane And John

It was Jane's turn to get up and make the coffee and John's turn to sleep in. Normally she would have got up quietly, tiptoed over to the closet, slipped into her robe, given John a kiss on the cheek and left the room, gently closing the door behind her. Not on this particular morning, however.

She'd got up on the wrong side of the bed. For some unexplained reason she'd been up half the night ruminating about her marriage and taking John's inventory. She thought about how he was never there for her, how he always took her for granted, how he spent every weekend watching football and how whenever she'd get upset with him, he'd accuse her of having her period. She thought about how he made her celebrate every holiday with his folks and how he never seemed to have any time for her family. Then came the *piece de resistance.* She thought about how he was always accusing her of being a spendthrift, insinuating that it was because of her they couldn't afford to get a nicer house.

Seeing as how it was because of John that she couldn't sleep, it was only fair that he should pay. So instead of doing the loving thing, which would have been to let him rest, she jerked her way out of bed, stumbled into the closet, put on her "ugly robe" and stomped out of the room, slamming the door behind her.

As planned, John was now wide awake and wondering what the heck was going on. He'd picked up on her covert messages and, to borrow a phrase, "the game was afoot." John began to think to himself: *"I wonder what I did wrong this time?"*

Hooked by his own co-dependent fears John leaped out of bed, threw on his pants and hurried down the hall toward the kitchen. When he got there, he found Jane peacefully sitting at the breakfast table reading the morning paper. He was about to ask what her problem was when she gazed up at him from behind the paper and in an innocent voice said, "Why John, what are you doing up?"

She loved turning the tables on him this way. She knew it made his computer smoke and left him hanging, but then that was the whole point of the exercise. John, on the other hand, was not a stupid man. He knew he was being toyed with and that she had sent him a mixed message. The problem was he just didn't know which message to believe.

John had grown up in a dysfunctional family where no one really said what they meant or meant what they said. Consequently he never learned to trust his feelings or listen to his own intuitions. So rather then make a mistake or risk a conflict, his normal M.O. was to play it safe and keep his mouth shut.

In the meantime, Jane had risen from the table, gone over to the sink and started washing the dishes. Once again John began to wonder if there was something wrong. Two things bothered him. First, he noticed that Jane was wearing her "ugly robe;" and second, he knew that she never did the dishes in the morning unless she was really upset. If he hadn't been so hooked into Jane's behavior, he might have been able to leave well enough alone. He would have, too, if Jane hadn't done such a good job of ignoring him. He hated it when she did that. It reminded him of how his mother used to treat him whenever he'd been a bad little boy. Jane knew how much this bugged John, but she had no intention of letting him off the hook. She had him right where she wanted him. Stubborn as he was, Jane knew he wouldn't be able to resist her ploy. After only five minutes of screaming silence, he broke down and asked her the burning question: "What's wrong with you?"

She turned around and said sweetly, "Nothing."

Her answer drove him crazy, and the child in his spirit ran around inside yelling, "She's lying! She's lying! Make her tell the truth!"

It took all the strength John had just to contain himself and keep his child from getting the best of him. Instead of losing control, which would have been to admit defeat, he decided to take the offensive and put Jane on the witness stand. *"Surely,"* he thought to himself, *"once I confront her with all the data, she'll have to confess."* So he climbed into his lawyer's garb and proceeded to cross-examine her.

John: Don't try and tell me that nothing's wrong. You don't go stomping around the house, slamming doors, washing dishes, wearing your ugly clothes and giving me the silent treatment unless there's something wrong. Am I right?

Sensing John's frustration, Jane decided to continue with her bait-and-switch routine. She let him finish and then she said,

Jane: What's wrong with you? What are you getting so upset about?

John: I'm not upset, and don't try to change the subject. I'm on to your little game and I'm telling you it won't work. You remind me of my mother. She was always playing mind games too.

Jane: John, I don't know what you're talking about. All I know is that one minute I was enjoying my morning and the next minute you're all over me.

John: I'm all over you? Now that's a joke. You've been on my case from the moment you first got up.

Jane: I'm concerned about you, John. You're acting like a crazy person.

John: *I'm* crazy, am I? Talk about the pot calling the kettle black. You've been on an emotional roller-coaster for as long as I've known you.

By this point in the game Jane is really beginning to feel some emotional relief. The little girl inside her is off in the corner laughing at John and saying to herself, *"We got him. We got him. Ha ha ha ha ha ha."* Then, to add insult to injury, Jane flashes a smile. John picks up on it right away:

John: Are you laughing at me? Is that a smile on your face? I suppose you think this is funny, don't you?

Jane: No, John, I don't think there's anything funny about the way you're acting.

John: The way I'm acting? Look at yourself, lady. God knows, I could have had lots of women. I don't know why I ever married you. Nothing I do is ever good enough for you.

Jane: I've never seen you like this, John. Are you sure you're feeling all right? Maybe you should go and see someone.

John: *I* should see someone! Look who's talking. You're the one who's always running around acting crazy. I'm just the poor fool who was dumb enough to get married to you.

I could go on, but to what end? We already know how this game turns out. Jane continues to deny her feelings and John continues to pick them up. Jane continues to feel better and John continues to feel worse. John experiences a tolerance break of the first order and Jane experiences vicarious relief.

The formula for passive aggression is simple: Take a co-dependent person who's angry and introverted about his or her feelings, sic them on another co-dependent person who's angry but extroverted about his or her feelings, leave them caged together for an extended period of time and let boil.

A close colleague of mine named Terry Kellogg compares the experience of passive aggression to being licked on the face by a big, beautiful dog while he empties his bladder on your foot. The point is that in the "maim game" of passive aggression there are two distinct sets of messages. One that says things are fine, and one that says they're not. Contradictory messages like these leave you feeling ambivalent inside — the way you might feel if your teenage daughter, after being out all night, came home and walked into the house at four in the morning holding a Gideon Bible in her hand. Think on that for a moment.

The best way to deal with someone who's playing a passive aggressive game is not to play. What this means is that when someone is being passive aggressive with you, you don't get hooked into doing their feelings for them. For example, in the case of Jane and John, it would have been a whole other story if John had simply walked away after Jane's first round of denial. She may have continued to be angry, but at least she would not have been able to get John to act out for her.

I wonder what might have happened on this particular occasion if John would have simply said to Jane, "Okay, honey, if you say there's nothing wrong, then there's nothing wrong. Anyway, I've got a lot of things to do today, so I think I'll make the best out of the morning and get an early start. Thanks for getting up and making the coffee. Hope you have a good day. I love you."

I know, you're thinking to yourself, "Easy to say, but not so easy to do." Agreed. Yet the fact is that nothing changes until something changes. Therefore, even if John's decision not to get hooked in would have made things worse, it would at least have brought about a definite change in the game. The critical point, then, is not so much *how* we first begin to change, but *that* we change. Remember, recovery is a matter of choice, not chance. The issue is progress in recovery, not perfection.

13

Who's Supposed To Be Driving My Bus?

Prior to the work of Freud and Berne, human nature was only defined in terms of a simple duality that consisted of a higher or superior self and a lower or inferior self. In theological terms this duality was often dramatized as an ongoing battle between the forces of good and evil — good representing God and evil representing the Devil. Freud and Berne, however, rejected this notion and predicted the existence of yet another dimension within our spirit. This dimension was not subject to the forces of good and evil, but reason. It was a cognitive, rational and logical self that distinguished us from all other forms of animal life and gave us the power to choose between right and wrong. In TA terms this dimension is the adult. And, in my opinion, it's our inner adult who should *always* be driving our bus.

Why *always?* Because it is our inner adult who possesses the ability to reason objectively through an issue, sort out fact from fiction and formulate a healthy resolution to our moral and emotional conflicts. This is not to suggest that our inner parent and child should be ignored or left out of the decision-making process. On the contrary, what I am proposing is simply a model of the inner family where our adult drives the bus and parent and child act as moral and emotional navigators, respectively.

Of course, in order to create this kind of cooperative intrapersonal relationship, our inner adult must be open to direction from our inner parent and child and competent in the areas of both moral logic (the ability to reason morally) and emotional logic (the ability to reason emotionally).

To better illustrate these two dimensions, let's imagine for a moment that you're involved in putting together a business deal that promises to be a real money-maker. There's only one catch. In order to come up with the money you need to fund the project, you'd have to steal it from your best friend.

Moral and emotional issues aside, pure logic might dictate that the shortest distance between two points is a straight line and that the end justifies the means. If, on the other hand, you were equipped to factor in all the moral and emotional issues, your logic would dictate that you put your friendship ahead of your desire for monetary gain.

The inability to exercise healthy moral and emotional boundaries is usually an indication of either co-dependency or a serious personality disorder. In the latter case the absence of healthy moral and emotional boundaries is due to a lack of conscience. Fortunately this is not the case with adult child/co-dependents, who do have a conscience and do experience healthy guilt and remorse whenever they compromise their own or someone else's moral or emotional boundaries.

The bad news is that the experience of healthy guilt and remorse alone is no guarantee that one would not continue to make the same mistakes over and over again. Repeating destructive patterns of behavior and continuing to violate one's moral and emotional boundaries in the process is a classic symptom of co-dependency. This condition, with respect to adult children and co-dependents, is yet another reflection of a delayed identity development syndrome fueled by an underdeveloped adult logic that is both morally and emotionally blind.

So it is not just an adult who should be driving our bus, but a mature adult who is competent to reason morally and emotionally as well. Ideally I am suggesting the presence of a compassionate adult logic that recognizes both the letter and the spirit of the law.

What About Having Fun?

One of the most frequently asked questions about the notion of an adult always driving the bus is, "How can our inner child have fun, be spontaneous, or play if there's always a logical gatekeeper standing in the way?"

To this I respond with a question of my own: "Would you let a child of yours go to an amusement park unsupervised?"

Inevitably, the answer is an emphatic "Absolutely not!"

When I ask, "Why not?" they reply, "because it would be wrong to leave a child alone in such a place and expect that he would not get into some kind of trouble."

On that point I always agree, and go on to explain that whether one is talking about young children or full-grown adults, healthy play requires healthy limits. The problem, then, is not the presence of adult supervision, but the lack of it.

Getting The Family Within To Work Together

In the previous section I talked about the relationship of moral and emotional logic and the role of our inner adult. In this section I want to expand on the discussion of our inner family and provide you with a description of how to develop a healthy style of circular communication between the parent, adult and child.

Before getting into the particulars of this discussion, let me take you back to our story about a child driving a two-ton bus down the highway. In this metaphor I asked you what you would do if you found yourself in the path of this bus from hell and I speculated that you'd immediately pull over. Assuming this to be the case, the next thing you might do is instinctively look to see if there was anyone else riding on the bus.

Now, this is where the story really gets good.

You glance over, and what do you see but two adult-looking passengers who seem totally oblivious to what's happening. One of them appears to be sleeping soundly, while the other is sitting calmly in the back of the bus reading a self-help book on adult children.

The sight sends a cold chill down your spine and you ask yourself, "Why aren't these two characters doing something to stop the child?"

You would never allow this to happen if you were sitting on that bus. Would you? "Of course not," you say emphatically. Still, we understand the metaphor and recognize the other characters riding on the bus as the inner parent and adult. The real quandary, then, is not who these people are, but why they fail to assert themselves and take back control of the bus.

The issue now is, how do we go about getting these different dimensions of our inner family to work together? By studying

1. During periods of noncon-flict the flow of inner dialogue is spontaneous and unob-structed.

2. In this state of rest there may be long periods of silence where no dialogue takes place.

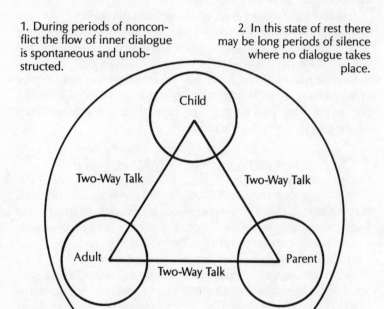

3. Under such conditions it is possible to have private con-versations between only two dimensions of the inner fami-ly: Adult and Child, Parent and Adult or Parent and Child.

4. Nonconflict periods offer an opportunity for our inner family to be alone together, relax and enjoy each other's company. In short, to heal.

NOTE: In all modes of circular communications the position of the parent, adult and child are never fixed. It is a fluid model based on the principles of balance, equality and mutual trust.

Figure 13.1. Circular Communications: Nonconflict Mode

1. During times of stress or conflict it is the job of our inner parent to care for our inner child's physical and emotional needs. Hugs, touches, words of affirmation and love are critical during such periods.

2. In addition to caring for the inner child it is the job of our parent to make sure that all relevant emotional and/or intuitive information from the child is passed on to the inner adult.

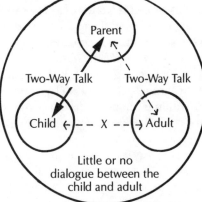

3. As always, the adult is busy driving the bus, assimilating information, processing data and making decisions. During periods of conflict there is little or no dialogue between the adult and child.

4. In these circumstances the child should be under the direct supervision of the parent and not allowed to distract the driver or get behind the wheel of the bus.

Figure 13.2.   Circular Communication: Conflict Mode

Figures 13.1 and 13.2 I believe you will begin to see ways in which we need to restructure the inner family and its dysfunctional patterns of communication.

The circular model, which I suggest you follow, has two basic operational modes. One is the inner family at rest (nonconflict), and the other is the family in conflict. Though there are several variations on this theme, these two modes best reveal the essence of this model.

Given the chronic patterns of avoidance that are so often associated with adult children and co-dependents during times of crisis, conflict or stress, this subject is worthy of a closer look. Let's use the analogy of a young couple and their seven-year-old child heading out on their first summer vacation together. Maybe you can recall going on one of these *National Lampoon* vacations yourself.

It starts out with Dad getting up at 4:30 A.M., loading up the car, hurrying everyone through breakfast and getting on the road by precisely 6 A.M. Within an hour of leaving home the child, who's been sitting alone on the back seat, begins to get restless. Dad is too busy driving to pay any attention.

The traffic on the freeway is backed up, there's a stalled car in the left lane and a construction crew is working on the right. Dad's patience is beginning to wear thin and Mom, who had never really woken up, is sleeping soundly.

Now about the time that Dad is ready to start honking the horn, the child leans forward, taps him on the shoulder and says, "I have to go to the bathroom really bad." That's all it takes for Dad to lose his temper, so he turns to the child and starts yelling. Frightened by his outburst, the child starts crying. This wakes Mom up and before you know it everyone in the car is screaming at one another. In all the commotion Dad takes his eyes off the road and almost rear ends the car in front of him.

Okay, what's wrong with this picture?

You're absolutely right. Dad, who is analogous to the adult dimension of the inner family, is being left to try and do it all. Mom, who is analogous to the inner parent, is neglecting her responsibilities as caretaker of the child and copilot to the adult. The kid in this story, who is analogous to the inner child, is being abandoned and neglected by both the inner parent and adult.

The child in this family is the only one who appears to be acting normally. Such would be the case for most children under these circumstances.

Here is how the dialogue might sound if we view the threesome in this example as actual members of a dysfunctional inner family:

Child to Adult: How much farther is it? I'm hungry. I have to go to the bathroom. I'm tired and I don't feel good. When are we going to get there? I'm bored. I miss my friends and I want to go home.

Parent: No comment.

Adult to Child: Can't you see I'm trying to drive? How do you expect me to concentrate when you're bugging me all the time? If you don't stop acting like a little brat and knock it off, I'm going to turn this car around and we won't go anywhere. I don't want to hear another peep out of you. If I do, there's going to be real trouble. Maybe I should stop right here and let you off. How does that sound?

Child to Adult: I hate you! [Starts crying.] You don't care about me. I wish I'd never been born!

Parent to Child: [A shaming look.] You better watch your mouth and stop all that crying or I'll give you something to cry about!

Adult to Child: I don't understand why you can't act more like an adult. Sometimes I wonder if you will ever grow up.

Adult to Parent: You know something? I'm beginning to wonder what his problem is. Some of the things he thinks and feels are really sick.

Parent to Adult: I agree. I've given up trying to deal with him. He's a real disappointment. God knows I've tried.

And so on and so on . . .

This is a fairly typical script for practicing adult child/co-dependents to have with themselves during periods of psychological and emotional stress. The child is the victim. His or her behavior may not elicit a positive response from the inner parent or adult, but it does elicit a response that is familiar. From the child's point of view even a negative response is better than no response at all.

Manipulating for attention is a predictable pattern for children whenever they feel that their physical, emotional and psychological security is being threatened. Shame and guilt, for example, can become familiar and even comforting to a child who knows little else. Finding comfort in such feelings is what I define in adult

child/co-dependents as their "Teddy bear of doom and gloom." I
have worked with many clients who actually fear the loss of their
shame. Remember, for someone who feels that they have nothing,
nothing can feel like something.

Fortunately there is a positive side to all this: We can recover
from an addiction to pain and suffering and heal the rift between
those members of our inner family. Below is an example of how
a healthy intrapersonal dialogue might sound under the conditions
previously outlined.

Adult to Parent: I would appreciate it if you would get with the
program here and pay some attention to our
kid. I can't drive and take care of him at the
same time.

Say It Like It Is

The parent and adult are competent to handle confrontation
between one another. Therefore, it is not so important how a
healthy message gets passed between them as it is that the
messages get passed. You can work on the style and quality of
their communications later. The first thing you need to do is
get them to say it like it is.

Parent to Adult: Sorry, I was off in my head somewhere. I apolo-
gize for leaving you hanging out there. I'll attend
to the kids so you can concentrate on the road.
Thanks for reminding me.

Parent to Child: Why don't I come back there with you so we can
spend some time together? Our adult is kind of
busy right now trying to get us through all this
heavy traffic.

Child to Parent: But I'm getting tired of being in the car and I
want to go home and be with my friends. I
thought we were going to have some fun. This
is boring!

Parent to Child: I know. Sometimes it's hard to sit and wait for
what we want. Well, at least we have each other.
Why don't we play a game or draw some pictures?

Child to Parent: Yeah! Let's draw some pictures together. I'll get
out my crayons and you can help me think of

	something to draw. When we finally get to the hotel, can I go to the pool and take a swim?
Parent to Child:	Sounds good to me. I think our adult might like that too. You're a neat kid and I love you a lot.
Adult to Parent:	Thanks for helping me out. I was really getting uptight trying to do two things at once. I really appreciate it when we all work together. By the way, a swim after we get settled sounds great.

In this script the inner parent and adult are both doing their jobs: The adult is attending to the business of driving, the parent is attending to the needs of the child and the child is getting to be a child. Logically, emotionally and morally the inner family is functioning as a healthy unit. There is balance, cooperation and mutual respect. Of course it is not always as easy to do as to say; but I want you to believe, as I do, that if you do the work to sort out these three dimensions of your inner family, you will, in time, be able to develop a healthy, proficient, spontaneous and mature style of both intrapersonal and interpersonal communication. The key is to start with yourself.

The Cunning, The Powerful And The Baffling

One day while I was giving a lecture to an audience of adult children/co-dependents on the structure of the inner family, the words *cunning, powerful* and *baffling* kept coming to mind. These familiar terms had long been used by those of us in AA and Al-Anon to describe the insidious nature of our disease. As I spoke it occurred to me that perhaps there was a relationship between these three dimensions of dependency and co-dependency and the three dimensions of our intrapersonal spirit.

I shared this thought with the audience and drew them a picture of how I saw these two sets of descriptive terms relating to one another. Figure 13.3 is a recreation of that first picture.

My view of parent as powerful, adult as cunning and child as baffling is, of course, a matter of subjective opinion. Nevertheless I believe these correlations do exist. The assignment of these terms and their relationship to one another were made through a logical translation of their literal meanings.

- Parent: moral self
- Powerful: moral efficacy

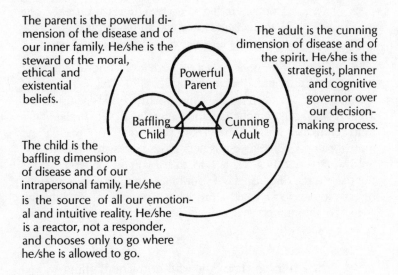

The parent is the powerful dimension of the disease and of our inner family. He/she is the steward of the moral, ethical and existential beliefs.

The adult is the cunning dimension of disease and of the spirit. He/she is the strategist, planner and cognitive governor over our decision-making process.

The child is the baffling dimension of disease and of our intrapersonal family. He/she is the source of all our emotional and intuitive reality. He/she is a reactor, not a responder, and chooses only to go where he/she is allowed to go.

Figure 13.3.   Cunning, Powerful And Baffling Map Of The Family Within

- Adult: fully matured
- Cunning: dexterous and crafty of mind
- Child: a person not yet of age
- Baffling: to defeat by confusing or puzzling

Labeling the child as powerful or cunning would be to assign him or her responsibility for choices that a child is morally and intellectually incompetent to make — buying a house, going to college, having children, getting married or driving a bus. It is true enough that children are good at manipulating the choices and decisions of our inner adult and parent, but they do not make the final decisions.

I believe that children go through any door that is left open to them, particularly if that door seems to lead away from potential pain or conflict. Furthermore, I do not believe that it is the child who opens or closes those doors of passage. The choice to leave a door open or unattended is the responsibility of a higher intellectual and moral entity, an adult or parent. Consequently, if our inner child lies, steals, runs away or somehow violates our personal or interpersonal boundaries, it is the inner parent and adult who must be held accountable.

Beyond the biophysical and/or genetic factors of addiction and compulsion, addiction is a disease that rests upon a *dis-ease.* I do not mean to suggest that co-dependency is the underlying cause of all addictions, but rather a fertile seedbed for many addictive and compulsive patterns of coping.

AA, Al-Anon And CoA: Metaphors Of The Family Within

The family of AA, Al-Anon and CoA offer yet another metaphorical representation of the intrapersonal family. More important, I came to see the growth and development of the 12-Step family as an analogy of the recovery process. Let me explain.

First, I thought about the history of AA and how, from its humble beginnings, it had grown into a fellowship with well over 10 million members. Then I thought about how this organization of supposedly helpless alcoholic men and women had gone about using this simple program to find a way into sobriety. Nothing fancy, just the simple logical and rational application of the 12 Steps. In this sense AA is the counterpart to our inner adult, that dimension of the spirit who has the cognitive and intellectual competence and cunning to lead the family through the moral and emotional conflicts of recovery.

Next, I thought about Al-Anon as the counterpart to our inner parent. This organization has helped millions of people detach from their obsessive role of caretaker and parent to adults who are acting like children. A co-dependent condition of chronic enabling that would ultimately lead them into a moral and ethical abandonment of self. So I think of Al-Anon as the inner parent of the 12-Step family and the one who is morally and ethically powerful enough to guide us through the dysfunctional parenting dilemmas of recovery.

Finally, I thought about CoA as the counterpart to our inner child. It is the newest member of the 12-Step family, and the organization whose job it is to help adult children and co-dependents confront their feelings and put a stop to over-reactive and compulsive patterns of coping. So it is that I see CoA as the counterpart to our inner child, as in the 12-Step family, and the place where healthy moral and intellectual direction is sought in order to work through the some-times confusing and emotionally baffling aspects of recovery.

When we combine the analogy outlined in this chapter with the one outlined in chapter 13, we come up with a unique perspective of how these issues relate to one another. Figure 14.1 is a diagram of this three-in-one model.

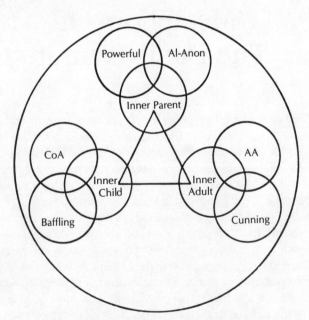

Figure 14.1. The Three-in-One Perspective

My integration of these three seemingly unrelated aspects of dis-ease, self-help and the family within are not mere contrivances. Over the centuries many writers, students and scholars of humanity and religion have speculated about the meaning of such three-dimensional themes in their work. It's my belief that they are all interrelated and collectively point to the existence of an existential relationship between human nature and the nature of the universe.

Whether you believe in this particular philosophy or not, it's difficult to deny the possibility that some type of abstract — or, for lack of a better term, spiritual — relationship does exist. This brings me to the fourth and final example of how the three-dimensional matrix operates within the discussion of our inner family.

Identity, Intimacy and Spirituality

To me the term spirituality means relationship. This relationship does not necessarily have to be with God, a Higher Power or some other deity; it may be a relationship to anything, animate or inanimate, that you hold as dear in life. Like the concept of identity and intimacy, the concept of spirituality is based on the assumption that it is through a process of open and honest communion within ourselves and with all of creation that we experience the ultimate sense of belonging, peace and purpose. So it is through the experience of these relationships, whatever they be, that we are able to form a spiritual sense of connection between ourselves and the universe at large.

The existence of our relationship to God or a Higher Power may not be as easy to define. Still, I believe that it is the establishment of an identity separate from those things outside of us that makes it possible for us to enjoy fully the experience of intimacy; and that it is during those moments of intimacy that we experience the presence of God or a Higher Power within.

Through this perspective I have come to believe that identity, intimacy and spirituality are related. Where there is identity, there is intimacy; where there is intimacy, there is spirituality and where there is spirituality, there is God. The concept of a Supreme Force or deity, then, is best defined in the presence of these three dimensions of the human experience. The search for identity, intimacy and spirituality is, in this sense, analogous to our search for God. The formula may be written as follows: Identity + Intimacy + Spirituality = God or Higher Power within. Figure 14.2 is my picture of how I see this.

Our sense of identity, intimacy and spirituality are all dimensions of relationship business. Each represents one aspect of the concept of a Higher Power. No one dimension is greater than the other, but there does seem to be an order that has to be followed. First is our

22222

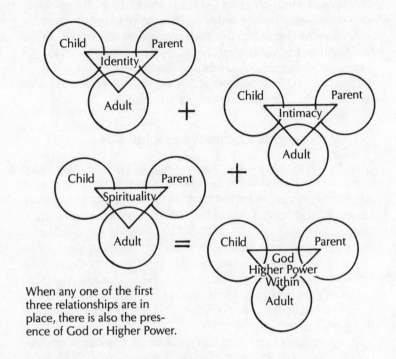

When any one of the first three relationships are in place, there is also the presence of God or Higher Power.

Figure 14.2.   Formula Of Identity, Intimacy, Spirituality And God Or Higher Power And The Family Within

need to know ourselves — this is identity. Second is our need to love unconditionally — this is intimacy. And third is our need to develop a trusting, honest and open relationship within ourselves — this is spirituality. By following this order we will eventually come to an understanding of identity, intimacy and spirituality with others and that Invisible Force that holds the universe together.

In light of this discussion let me ask you a couple of simple questions:

Question 1: If a flaming adult child/co-dependent were to pray in earnest to his or her God or Higher Power for help in recovery, to which member of the intrapersonal family do you think He or She or It would speak first? The inner parent, adult or child?

Answer: The inner child.

Question 2: Why the inner child instead of the inner parent?

Answer: Because the unhealthy inner parent is confused and believes he or she is God or a Higher Power. In such cases God/Higher Power would probably say to He or She or Itself, "I cannot talk to this person because this person thinks he or she is Me."

Question 3: Why not the inner adult then?

Answer: Because the unhealthy inner adult would not believe the person speaking was really God/Higher Power. Being intellectually dysfunctional, he or she would more than likely ask God/Higher Power for some I.D., to which God/Higher Power would probably say, "I do not have to prove who I Am, because I Am."

So it is that God/Higher Power chooses to speak to the child in our spirit because he or she is the only one who is open, trusting and loving enough to listen. Thank heaven we have someone inside our spirit who is receptive to that which passes all our worldly understanding.

Making A Better Life

There was a time early on in my recovery when I felt the need to confront my parents about all the mistakes I thought they'd made while I was growing up. It was not something I wanted to do, it was something I thought I had to do. I just assumed, like so many of my adult child/co-dependent counterparts, that it was what I had to do in order to recover. So I impulsively decided to visit my folks and have a heart-to-heart with them.

It was an interesting experience, but not exactly the one I was hoping for. Nonetheless it was not a total loss, and if nothing else, I did gain a deeper understanding of and appreciation for who they were and how they came to be that way.

As products of World War I and the Great Depression, both my parents had grown up in the shadows of a stoic survivalist tradition. Consequently, when I broached the subject of my childhood, the first thing they told me was, "We did the best we could with the tools we had and we worked damn hard to make a better life for you."

I immediately felt a sense of guilt and shame for ever having thought to question them. At the same time my inner child felt angry, hurt and resentful that they were still unwilling to admit to any wrongdoing.

Obsessed as I was with trying to get what I'd come for, my inner parent and adult told me that this was not the time or place to pursue the subject. It was their opinion that discretion would be the better part of valor, and so they gathered up my inner child and together we gracefully took our leave of them.

For days afterwards, however, my inner family continued to talk about what had happened. Despite all the negative thoughts and feelings, I knew inside that actually my parents had, through all their mistakes, managed to build a better life for me. I just knew that intuitively this was true. Though nothing had really changed on the outside, I realized that something had changed on the inside. For the first time in my adult life I felt the familiar knot of emotional pain begin to loosen in my stomach.

My inner child seemed to take comfort in the idea that all was not lost and that there was still much to look forward to. Surprisingly, there were even some healing words from my inner parent who said, "Morally, I think it would be right for us to let go of our negative thoughts and feelings about Mom and Dad. I think we need to accept the fact that they aren't perfect and begin to see them for what they really are — human beings. I vote we stop trying to change them and start changing ourselves. This is not to say that we should forget what happened, but rather that we should begin to let go of what happened."

"I second the motion," said my inner adult.

"And I third the motion," said my inner child.

Before the meeting was adjourned, we all decided that it was time for us to move on and begin taking advantage of the better life our parents had made for us. Most important, we all agreed that it was our responsibility now for whatever happened in our life.

Difficult as this passage may be to make, I would encourage you, the reader, to see the wisdom in it and begin to do likewise. I'm not suggesting that you should forget or even forgive what happened to you as a child. I am suggesting that you sit down with yourself and, through a round-table discussion, begin to develop a plan that will enable you to let go and grow. Turning your liabilities into assets is a process that requires the participation of all three parts of your inner family.

You need to do this at your own pace and in your own time, but sooner or later it will have to be done. Whether you are able to forgive or not, you still need to let go. No matter how bad it was or continues to be, I want you to believe that the worst is already behind you. You've come too far to give up the battle now.

As Bill H.L., a recovering co-dependent lawyer friend of mine once said, *"Illegitimi non carborundum"* — or, loosely translated, "Don't let the past grind you down."

Healing your family within does not require you to mend the relationship with your parents or even forgive them. Nor does it require that they themselves ever recover. What matters is that you mend the torn relationships of your spirit and recover from the inside out. In this way you will find the strength and courage you need to go on and build a better life for yourself and your children.

Remember, you are dealing with co-dependency — cunning, powerful and baffling — a dis-ease from which no one recovers alone. To paraphrase a section of chapter 5 from the Big Book of Alcoholics Anonymous, I beg you to be fearless and thorough from the very start, and remember that half measures will avail you nothing.

I hope you have begun to understand the core dimensions of your own intrapersonal family and are ready to begin the recovery process. For the remainder of this book we will learn the how-tos of healing your family within.

PART FOUR

Recovering
Your Inner Family

On The Road to Recovery:
Donna's Story

About a year ago I started counseling a young woman named Donna, who had come to me for help with her adult child/co-dependency issues. Not long into the process she began to share with me how, as an adolescent, she had been sexually abused by her older brother and several of his friends. It was a memory that she had buried but not forgotten.

As I listened to her talk about this painful chapter in her life, it became evident to me that her inner child was being emotionally and psychologically battered by her sick inner adult, who was trying to guilt her into dismissing the entire incident. At the same time I could see her inner parent trying to shame her into thinking that everything that had happened was her fault. Clearly Donna's inner child was caught between a mountain of guilt and an ocean of shame.

I started to work with Donna right away on developing a mental image of her inner family so that she might begin to understand how her inner adult and parent were abusing the child in her spirit. Figure 15.1 is a map of Donna's inner family as I described them to her.

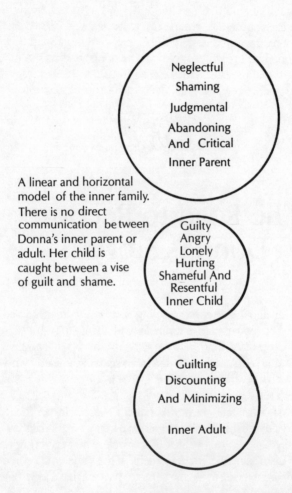

A linear and horizontal
model of the inner family.
There is no direct
communication between
Donna's inner parent or
adult. Her child is
caught between a vise
of guilt and shame.

Neglectful

Shaming

Judgmental

Abandoning
And Critical

Inner Parent

Guilty
Angry
Lonely
Hurting
Shameful And
Resentful
Inner Child

Guilting
Discounting
And Minimizing

Inner Adult

**Figure 15.1.   Donna's Map Of Her Inner Family
After Two Months Of Therapy**

Slowly Donna began to see how she had become her own worst enemy and how her inner child had been placed in a no-win situation. As the discovery process continued, Donna began to confront the dysfunctional patterns of her inner family and let go of the toxic legacy of shilt that she had inherited from her family of origin. With each successive confrontation Donna was able to recall more and more about the details of her past. Six months into her journey Donna had broken through all the denial and was talking freely about the abuse she had suffered from her brother. As she peeled away the layers of denial, she also began to get in touch with her inner child and the way her inner parent and adult had abandoned the child — just as her mom and dad had done. She saw how she needed to stop running, confront her brother and reclaim her personal power.

I told her that the day would probably come when she would have to confront this man, but that today was not the day. "When you're ready," I said to her, "your inner child will let you know." I didn't want Donna to guilt or shame her child into doing something that she was not prepared to do. I told her I believed her inner child would be ready only after it was clear to her that she didn't have to do it alone.

She understood, and for the next several months we focused on two issues. First, we wanted to help her inner child feel safe; and second, we wanted to get her inner parent and adult to start caring for the child.

Finally it happened. Donna came and announced to me that she had met with her brother and confronted him about the sexual abuse. I could tell from the sound of her voice and the look on her face that it had been a difficult but successful encounter. So, for the better part of that session, I just sat and listened as she shared her story. This was one of those rare occasions in counseling where you could actually see the healing process taking place. It was a real privilege to watch, and an experience that I will not soon forget.

Because of how dramatically Donna's story illustrates the process of healing the family within, I decided to ask her if she would allow me to share her story with you. She gave me her permission and expressed her wish that it might serve as a source of hope and inspiration to other adult child/co-dependents who are on the road to recovery.

In Donna's Words

It was two weeks ago, on a Tuesday morning, that I decided to contact my brother and set up a meeting with him. From the moment I started to think about it, my inner child was busy trying to talk me out of doing it. I told her that everything would be okay, that I would not abandon her, but I don't think she really believed me. I mean, she didn't exactly have that much confidence in either my inner adult or parent to be there for her.

Anxious as my little girl was, I didn't let her drive my bus. With my heart in one hand and the phone in the other, my inner adult picked up the receiver and dialed my brother's number. He must have been about to place a call himself because he answered almost before it had a chance to ring. He said, "Hello?" For an instant I thought seriously about hanging up. But I didn't. I said, "Hello, this is your sister, Donna." He acknowledged that it was me, but I could tell from the tone of his voice that he was not glad to hear from me. I went on anyway, and told him that I really wanted to see him, that I needed to talk with him about some personal issues. He asked if we could do it over the phone instead. I told him that I did not want to do that and asked again if he wouldn't consider coming over to my house so we could talk face-to-face.

Then in an angry voice, he asked, "What's this all about? What's so important and personal that we can't talk about whatever it is over the phone?"

My inner child was shaking with fear, but I maintained my composure and my adult answered him. "I really don't want to talk about it over the phone. And as I said before, what I would prefer is for you to come over to my house so that we can talk one-to-one. Sunday around noon would be great . . . if it would be convenient for you."

(Earlier in our counseling together I had told Donna that if and when she ever did decide to talk to her brother, it would be to her advantage to do so at a time and place of her choosing. A time when she was rested and a place where she felt strong.)

After a rather long pause he said, "Fine, I'll be over at noon on Sunday," and hung up without saying goodbye.

That was Tuesday, and by Saturday night I was feeling physically ill from all the emotional anxiety and stress that I was carrying around inside. By Sunday I had worked myself into such a state that I was literally on the verge of throwing up.

Then came the knock at the door. My little girl was as scared as she could be, but my inner adult just kept telling her that he was not going to hurt us and that things would turn out all right. He came into the house. He looked angry. He followed me into the den, where I had decided I wanted us to talk. He stated that he had another commitment and couldn't stay long. It was clear to me that he was not in a good mood and that he did not want to be there. He left his sunglasses on and stared out of the window. I wanted to say something to him, but I couldn't find the words. I could feel my stomach tensing up as I sat there. I started to feel sick to my stomach. I heard my little girl tell me that she was going to throw up.

I told my brother that I didn't really feel very well and excused myself. I hurried to the bathroom and immediately got sick. As I slumped over the toilet gagging, I had the distinct feeling that I was standing outside of my body watching myself. I didn't remember much else about what went on while I was in there. I guess I must have cleaned myself up, because the next thing I knew I was back in the den sitting on the couch. My brother was still looking out the window, waiting for me to speak.

I asked him if he wanted a cup of coffee, but he said he didn't want anything and sat down on the other end of the couch. After a moment he turned and faced me, but not a word came out of his mouth. I continued to have the feeling that I was standing outside of myself, but when I stopped to think about it, it seemed like I was back inside my body again. It was like being in one minute and out the next. It wasn't a bad feeling; in fact it actually made me feel kind of good. It was in the middle of one of these in/out fluctuations that I saw my inner child for the first time. It was as if she had stepped right out of my skin and took up a position leaning against the oak table that sits in front of the couch. She stood there motionless, facing us.

She was about four or five, and wearing a red dress exactly like the one I used to have as a child. She didn't speak, she simply stood there looking at me. I was so taken aback by the vision that I literally forgot about my brother.

He must have sensed that I had gone off somewhere in my head because he started to speak. As I turned to look at him, I noticed that he was hitting the arm of the couch with his fist. I think he was trying to get my attention, but my mind was on the little girl. So I looked back again to see if she was still standing by the table.

As I did I heard my brother say, "I don't know what you want from me, Donna, but I hope it's not about trying to build a relationship with me because I don't know if that's possible. You see, Donna, the truth is I don't even like you. In fact, I've hated you ever since I was in high school."

Obviously it wasn't something that I wanted to hear, but it was what I expected. I felt both hurt and relieved at the same time. Somewhere inside I had always known that he felt that way.

I asked him why he hated me and he said, "You want to know why? All right, I'll tell you. It started when Mom used to make me take you everywhere I went. You were always getting in my way. I hated you because you always accomplished what you said you were going to do. You're the successful one in the family, and you always get what you want. Because you think you're so wonderful and because my children like you so much. I guess, in short, it's because I'm jealous of you."

I sat there for a moment, and then I felt my child step away from the table. She moved forward and stopped about half-way between my brother and me. She didn't seem afraid of anything. It was more like she had moved to get a better view of us both. I think she was studying me, but I'm not sure.

At that point I decided it was time to tell my brother what it was that I had to say. I started out by telling him that I appreciated his honesty about how he felt and that it didn't really come as any surprise. Then I told him that I had a few things of my own to share.

I heard my inner adult remind me of what I'd learned in therapy — namely that I was not there to talk about my brother's stuff, but about my own stuff. My mission was not to attack him, but to reclaim my own personal power. In other words it was not for his benefit that I was sharing, but for my own. I was there to confront my own fears, stand up for myself and embrace that part of my spirit that I had left behind as a child.

With that, I began to tell him how I had been sexually abused as a child and how I needed to share that experience with him. He looked at me and said, "Who sexually abused you?" I paused for a second, and out of the corner of my eye I saw my inner child staring at me. She didn't have to say anything, I could tell from the look on her face that she was wondering what I was going to say.

I looked back at my brother and said, "You did." He just sat there and stared at me. I asked him if he remembered when he and his friends used to take me out in the back yard or in the tent fort and touch me, look at me and hurt me.

His whole demeanor changed. A solemn look came over his face and he said to me, "You don't have to say anymore, I remember."

I could hardly believe it. It was as if he had just lifted a huge weight off my shoulders. I felt like a whole person for the first time in my life. I looked once more to see my child, but she was gone. I started to scan the room to find her, when suddenly I felt her standing right next to me. I know how strange this sounds, but I could tell from the way she was acting that she was beginning to trust me. I sensed that she wasn't afraid anymore. We looked at each other for a moment and then, without a word, she climbed up into my lap, leaned back in my arms and melted into my body.

My brother had been talking this whole time, and when I finally got myself tuned back into what he was saying, I realized that he had moved on to another subject. He had shifted the focus from him and me to talking about how he, too, had been sexually abused by two teenage boys when he was only five. It was obvious that he had some of his own issues to deal with, but I was in no position to help him. I was too busy just trying to deal with my own stuff.

As I listened to him, though, I began to notice that he was slipping back into his old angry self. Whatever the brief connection had been between us, it was gone. To underscore this point he turned to me and said, "This doesn't change anything. I can't tell you that one talk on a Sunday afternoon is going to change how I feel toward you."

I asked him again why he hated me so. This time he told me that it was because he had always seen me as the one in the family who could do no wrong, the one who got good grades, the one who was clearly Mom's favorite and the one who went out into the world and succeeded at everything she did. Not because of any special treatment I had received, but because, as he put it, I always seemed to go out and get what I wanted. He said it was because of my talents that Mom was always comparing him to me and judging him as inferior.

I was amazed at his recounting of the past. It was like we had both been living out the same script. I told him that as a little girl, I had felt like the inferior one and that I had always seen him as the smart one, the one who always got what he wanted, the one who was Mom's favorite. I went on to tell him that I had always thought of myself as the ugly duckling. Then I heard myself say something to him that I had never thought of before. I told him that I had always seen him as my only link to Mom, that I'd always believed that if I could get him to like me then maybe Mom would like me too.

This was a powerful revelation for me. I realized that I had stumbled into a painful truth about my past. I began to understand that my fear of losing my relationship with my brother was really my fear of losing my relationship with my mother.

It all seemed to make perfect sense. Mom had played my brother and me off one another. In the process she had pitted my brother and me against each other. As a result my brother had come to hate me and I had come to fear my brother. For the first time I could see how our feelings about each other were really feelings that had to do with our relationship to Mom.

By this time my brother was beginning to edge his way toward the front door. I remained seated on the couch. At that point I was only half aware of his even being in the house. I found myself thinking again about my inner child, and as I did, she suddenly reappeared. This time she was sitting right beside me on the couch. There were tears running down her cheeks and a needy look on her face, so I put my arms around her and just held her.

Then I heard my brother say that he was leaving and that he wasn't sure that he wanted to ever talk with me again, or where this relationship was headed. I didn't care much either way, so I said nothing. He looked at me for a moment, turned around and walked out the door. I sat there holding my child and just stared out the window. I felt good inside about what had happened. It seemed as though I was finally at peace with myself.

Then, unannounced, my brother came back into the den. He stood in front of me and said, "I'm so sorry that I was ever a part of anything that hurt someone so badly." I knew deep inside that he was genuinely sorry about having abused me and that if nothing else, we had both experienced some healing that day.

The Missing Inner Parent

Donna's encounter with her brother marked the beginning of her journey toward healing her inner family. I asked her what she had discovered about the relationship between her inner parent, adult and child as a result of this dramatic episode.

"First of all," she said, "I've come to really see my inner child. I know now that it was not her fault and that feels great. Secondly, I got in touch with my inner adult and have learned that she has the ability to face my conflicts and not get overwhelmed by all the fear. Third, I sense that my little girl is no longer feeling alone, she is really beginning to feel like she isn't alone anymore. And the last thing I am beginning to see is that, as quick as my inner parent is to judge and criticize my inner child, she was nowhere to be found when it came to caring for or nurturing my child."

I told Donna that her insight about her inner parent was important, and that in order to recover completely, there was much work that needed to be done with her inner parent. I told her that because of all the dysfunctional parenting we had been exposed to as children, we often grew up knowing little about how to be good to ourselves.

Because of this, I told her, inner parents are typically the last members of our family within to join the recovery process. This is because they have absolutely no understanding of their role as parent to the child in our spirit. While they seem to know a lot about their moral and ethical responsibilities as a parent to children on the outside, they don't seem to understand that these same principles apply to their job as parent to the inner child.

Becoming Your
Own Good Parent

When adult child/co-dependents tell me that they don't know how to be a good parent to themselves, I present them with the following scenario:

Pretend that you're strolling down the sidewalk of a busy street. Up ahead, you see a small child sitting on the curb crying. What are you going to do? Right! You go up to the child, kneel down, give a re-assuring smile, and in a gentle voice ask if he or she needs any help.

Good plan. You're being a good parent-type person. Now the child says to you, "I'm lost. I can't find my mommy, and I know she's going to be really mad." Then you say, "Don't worry, things are going to be just fine, and I'll stay with you until we find your mommy."

Nice job! You're doing everything right.

Now, because of the great job you've done, the child lets go completely, throws his or her arms around you, and asks "Do you love me?" The question catches you off guard, but you don't hesitate. Like the good parent you are, you say, "Yes, I love you!"

Excellent! Terrific! Fantastic! You've passed the most important test of all. You've given the child the only thing he or she needed to hear.

After walking adult child/co-dependents through this imaginary drama, it is no longer a question of whether they know how to be good parents. They do. The critical issue now is whether they recognize the child in this story as the child in their own spirit. I tell them that their ability to care for the child in this story is hardly an indication of their incompetence as a parent. Then I say, "I understand how you may never have thought of parenting yourself this way, but I cannot support the idea that you are incapable of being a good parent to your own inner child."

Confronting the delusional belief system of the adult child/co-dependent's inner parent may be a difficult task but it is a necessary part of the healing process. For too long we have excused our inner parent on the basis that he/she was ignorant, or that their treatment of our inner child was justified because of their belief that the inner child was not like other children. This is an unacceptable defense.

How terrible it must be for our inner child to watch us give to others the love they need and want so badly. Worse yet, we gave this love to people who often didn't want, need or even deserve the gift we were giving — to an adult or spouse, for example, who was acting like a child. It's a child's logic that believes that by always loving others we will be able to get them to love us back. This was the logic I learned growing up and because of it, I routinely abandoned myself in my relationships with others.

Stop Making Excuses

So, before I could recover, I had to learn to stop making excuses for my inner parent and start holding him accountable for his part in my dis-ease. I had to get him to stop abusing my inner child and see the error of his ways. In short, I needed to get him to stop withholding his love and start being a good parent to my inner child.

To help Donna begin this process I gave her a picture of how the dysfunctional inner parent looks in relationship to the inner child. Typically, I told her, there are three basic types of dysfunctional inner parenting: The inconsistent inner parent, the consistently over-inflated inner parent and the consistently absent inner parent.

The inner parent depicted in Figure 16.1A is overly involved to the point where the inner child feels incompetent and can do nothing for him/herself. In this position the inner parent may be trying to help, but ends up doing too much.

Then, for no apparent reason, the inner parent may all but disappear, leaving the relationship to look like Figure 16.1B. In this position the inner child gets no direction, love or support, and

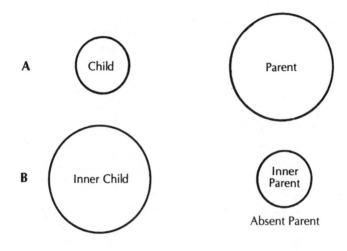

Figure 16.1. The Inconsistent Inner Parenting Model

winds up feeling abandoned, frightened and alone. Through this inconsistent model the inner child develops a private logic that says, "The only thing for sure is that nothing is for sure." This is perhaps the most destructive model of parental behavior because it creates a chronic sense of mistrust within the child. Even consistently critical or neglectful parenting would be less debilitating to the child. At least then the child would know what to expect.

In Figure 16.2 the inner parent is always overinflated and cuts the child no quarter. He or she is consistently uncaring, judgmental and shaming toward the inner child. The result of this consistently abusive and overbearing inner parenting is that the inner child never feels protected or cared about.

In Figure 16.3 the child learns that he or she is totally without support. In both good times and bad, the inner child comes to feel as though he or she is unworthy of being loved or cared for by anyone.

In Donna's case Figure 16.1 tells the story. When things were just going along, her inner parent was overinflated and constantly preach-

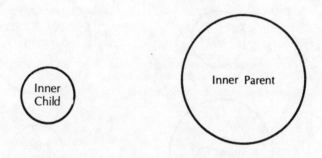

Figure 16.2. The Consistently Overinflated Inner Parenting

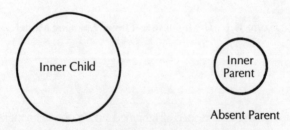

Figure 16.3. The Consistently Absent Inner Parent

ing to her inner child about her incompetence. Then when things got hard or a conflict arose, her inner parent would disappear and leave her inner child to cope with the situation by herself.

As we talked about this inconsistent and dysfunctional pattern of her inner parent, Donna began to share with me a dream that she had been having. She told me that in the dream her inner child would come to her and take her down a long corridor to what she thought was a hospital room. Once inside, she said, her little girl would lead her over to a bed where there was a sick person plugged in to all sorts of life-support systems. She said that she thought she should know the person, but that she could not seem to make out the face.

When she finished telling me about the dream, she asked me if I had any ideas about who the little girl was taking her to see. I said to her that I thought I did, but that it was something she would have to decide for herself. With that we ended the session and arranged for her to come in again in a couple of weeks. When she returned, she had the answer. She told me that it was her inner parent, and that the person whom her inner child had been leading down the hall was her inner adult. At that point I smiled and told her that I thought the same thing.

She asked "What does my inner child want my adult to do?" I responded, "What do you think she wants?" Donna replied, "I think my little girls wants my adult to do something to help my inner parent." I said, "That sounds right to me."

So began phase two of Donna's journey toward recovering her inner family. Her little girl had turned to her inner adult for help. As is the case for most adult child/co-dependents in recovery, it is the inner adult who must ultimately take the lead in confronting the dysfunctional patterns of a sick inner parent. Only the inner adult has the intellectual strength and courage to deal with abusive, neglectful and shaming behavior patterns of an overinflated parental ego.

For Donna it was a matter of getting the inner adult to recognize the problem and begin using her logic to help revive and rehabilitate the inner parent. From that day on Donna was no longer feeling incompetent to make the changes she needed to make. Together we practiced defining the different things that her inner adult could do and say that would help the parent recover. Her first dialogue between her inner adult and parent went something like this:

Adult to Parent: Hello there. I've come to help you get back on your feet. It's time we both started to get with the program. Like me, I know you've been at a loss as to what to do. Well, I'm not as lost as I once was, and I know that I can't do what needs to be done alone. Our inner child needs both of us.

Parent to Adult: But I'm sick and tired of trying to get the kid in us to be the kind of person I was told she ought to be.

Adult to Parent: I know it's confusing, but what they taught us about her was wrong. It's not our little girl who's bad, it's the logic and <u>rules</u> we learned that are bad. I've begun to see that, and the only way out of this mess is for us to emancipate ourselves from that legacy of lies and define our own set of rules for living together as a family.

Parent to Adult: That sounds fine, but how do we go about making our little girl understand that it's not right for her to feel and think the way she does?

Adult to Parent: That's the first rule you have to change. It's not our child's thoughts and feelings that are the problem, it's our inability to accept her as she is. She's only acting normally, considering where we came from and how we treat her.

Parent to Adult: Are you telling me that I'm being a bad parent?

Adult to Parent: Yes, I am saying that, but I'm not putting all the blame on you. I haven't exactly been doing a great job myself.

Parent to Adult: Who appointed you God?

Adult to Parent: Maybe if you weren't so busy playing God yourself, you could understand what I'm saying to you. All I need you to know for now is that I will not tolerate your abuse of our child anymore. All you need to do right now is get up out of that bed and take a seat in the back of the bus. Maybe in time you will come to see what your job in this family is.

Parent to Adult: Fine, but don't expect any help from me.

Adult to Parent: Fortunately, I'm not alone. I have a counselor, an ACoA group and some other recovering friends to parent me while you are still unable to do your job.

This first conversation was far from the idyllic fantasy that Donna wanted to hear, but it was an honest one and a good beginning. I

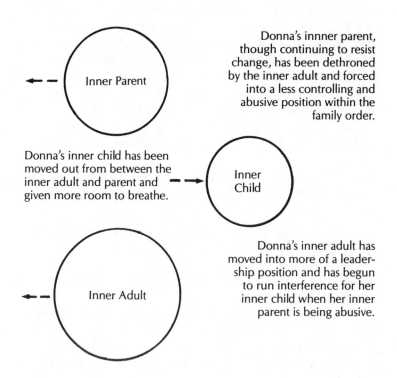

Donna's innner parent, though continuing to resist change, has been dethroned by the inner adult and forced into a less controlling and abusive position within the family order.

Donna's inner child has been moved out from between the inner adult and parent and given more room to breathe.

Donna's inner adult has moved into more of a leader-ship position and has begun to run interference for her inner child when her inner parent is being abusive.

Figure 16.4.   Donna's Map Of Her Inner Family After Six Months Of Therapy

told her that the resistance of her inner parent was not unusual considering the long history of dysfunctional parenting that she had grown up with. I assured Donna, as I have many adult child/co-dependents, that given enough time and help her inner parent would eventually come around. The important thing for her to remember now was that her inner child was no longer alone and that it was not her job to drive the bus or try to fix the inner parent.

To give you a clearer picture of how Donna's progress looked on the inside, I would ask you to refer back to Figure 15.1, the initial map of Donna's inner family, and compare it to Figure 16.4.

Clearly Donna has much more work to do before her inner family will reach a healthy state of psychological, moral and emotional balance. The primary challenge for Donna now is to be patient and continue to trust in the process.

My Mother, My Father, Myself

Donna's successful encounter with her brother gave her the courage and understanding she needed to begin emancipating herself from the dysfunctional parenting scripts of her past. For Donna this meant taking an honest, fearless and searching inventory of herself and her relationship to her parents.

To start this process I had Donna put together two lists of all the covert (unspoken) and overt (spoken) rules that she had learned from her parents — one list for the rules she learned from her mother, and one for the rules she learned from her father. On the left side I asked her to list what she considered to be the healthy rules, and on the right I asked her to list all the unhealthy rules.

The purpose of this exercise is threefold. First, to have Donna see both sides of the story; second, to keep her from throwing out the baby with the bathwater; and third, to help her inner parent, adult and child identify the specific rules they need to change.

Here are some of the rules that Donna came up with:

Rules From Dad

Healthy Rules	Unhealthy Rules
1. (unspoken) Dads are good to their kids.	1. (unspoken) Men don't show feelings.

2. (spoken) People have to work for what they want.
3. (spoken) Honesty is the best policy.
4. (spoken) Look before you leap.
5. (spoken) Waste not, want not.
6. (spoken) Kids should be kids.
7. (spoken) Education is important.
8. (spoken) Love one another.

2. (unspoken) Boys are more important than girls.
3. (unspoken) Women are objects.
4. (spoken) Don't trust anyone.
5. (spoken) Always put the needs of others first.
6. (spoken) You made your bed, now sleep in it.
7. (spoken) Kids should be seen and not heard.
8. (unspoken) Showing affection is not okay.

Rules From Mom

Healthy Rules

1. (spoken) Family is important.
2. (spoken) God loves little children.
3. (spoken) Always tell the truth.
4. (spoken) Develop your talents.
5. (spoken) Good grooming is important.
6. (spoken) Do unto others as you would have them do unto you.
7. (spoken) Put your trust in God.
8. (spoken) Be forgiving and merciful to others.

Unhealthy Rules

1. (spoken) Always put your family ahead of yourself.
2. (spoken) Don't ever be selfish.
3. (spoken) God hates a sinner.
4. (unspoken) A woman's place is in the home.
5. (spoken) Life is only happy in the hereafter.
6. (unspoken) Sex is dirty.

7. (unspoken) Men are better than women.
8. (spoken) Don't talk about the family secrets.

What Donna Learned

Once Donna had completed her inventory of the rules she had learned from her parents, I asked her to draw a map of how she imagined her mom's and dad's inner families might have looked based on these rules. Figure 16.5 and 16.6 shows what she drew.

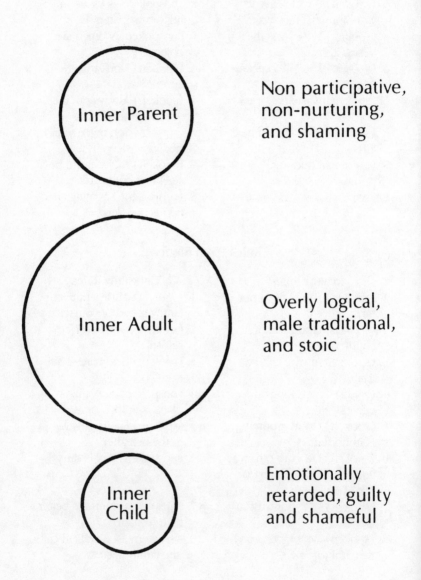

Figure 16.5. Donna's Map Of Her Dad's Inner Family

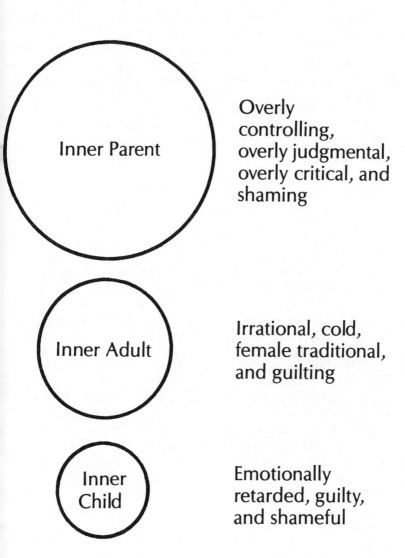

Inner Parent — Overly controlling, overly judgmental, overly critical, and shaming

Inner Adult — Irrational, cold, female traditional, and guilting

Inner Child — Emotionally retarded, guilty, and shameful

Figure 16.6. Donna's Map Of Her Mom's Inner Family

When Donna had finished putting together all the information she had gathered from these two exercises, it was painfully clear to her how she had come to be so hard on herself. She had spent most of her childhood trying to live up to overt and covert expectations of an overinflated adult logic and parental morality. The most obvious consequence of all this was that Donna had never been allowed to be a child. The end result was that she wound up abandoning herself in an effort live up to the unhealthy rules and expectations of her parents. It was a no-win situation. When she tried to be a child, she was told to be more like an adult, and when she tried to be an adult, she got treated like a child.

When faced with the inevitable meaning of all this — that she would have to break out of her dysfunctional relationship to her parents — the old co-dependent logic and fear of her childhood came rushing back. To challenge the authority of her parents would mean to break with co-dependent tradition; and to break with tradition would mean to break the rules; and to break the rules would mean to be abandoned; and to be abandoned would mean to be left alone and to be left alone would be to die.

This line of thinking was, of course, the immature logic of Donna's inner child. It was, however, never more apparent to her how this logic had continued to victimize her as an adult. Even as an adult Donna's inner child was still trying to live up to her parents' expectations.

"At long last," Donna said, "I see that it is not a matter of whether I ever confront my folks. I mean, confronting them doesn't necessarily mean that anything would change inside me. The parent I need to confront is the one who lives in my spirit. She's the one who's abusing, neglecting and abandoning me now. I can see, too, that it's not my inner child's responsibility to confront my sick parent. It's the job of my inner adult."

From this point on Donna really began to take the lead in her own recovery. Her inner adult was clearly on the mend. Her inner child was beginning to relax emotionally; and her inner parent, although still resisting change, was no longer being allowed to play God. All things considered, I'd say that Donna had turned the corner and was well on her way to healing her family within. As of our last meeting, Donna saw her inner family as shown in Figure 16.7.

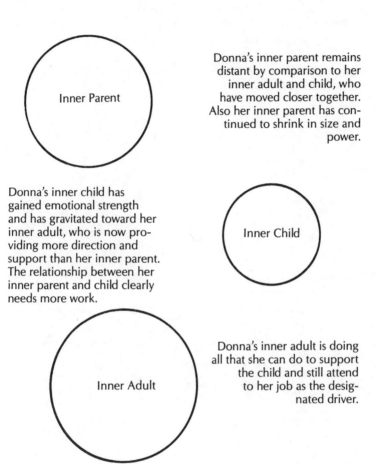

Donna's inner parent remains distant by comparison to her inner adult and child, who have moved closer together. Also her inner parent has continued to shrink in size and power.

Donna's inner child has gained emotional strength and has gravitated toward her inner adult, who is now providing more direction and support than her inner parent. The relationship between her inner parent and child clearly needs more work.

Donna's inner adult is doing all that she can do to support the child and still attend to her job as the designated driver.

Figure 16.7. Donna's Map Of Her Inner Family After Eight Months Of Therapy

Healthy Inner Dialogue

Once upon a time there was a man who decided that he would try and write a book about his experiences as a recovering alcoholic, adult child and co-dependent. It seemed like a good idea at the time. Logically he told himself that it would be good for his career and that there was really nothing to fear. The worst-case scenario was that he wouldn't find a publisher and all his time and energy would have been for naught. The best-case scenario was that he'd find a publisher, people would buy his book and he'd discover that others actually thought he had something worthwhile to say.

So with the strength of his conviction and an optimistic attitude, he sat down at his word processor and began to write. He had no clear sense of how long the whole project would take, but he was confident that within a year he'd be able to complete the first rough draft.

Unfortunately this was not to be. The days turned into weeks, the weeks turned into months and by the end of the first year he had barely got through half the manuscript.

About this time his wife had begun to ask him how it was going. He knew she deserved a straight answer, but he also knew that her patience was beginning to wear thin. So he put her off as best he could. Eventually, however, she did get him to 'fess up and, as predicted, she was not at all sympathetic. It had become such a bone of contention between them that by the middle of the second year, she was unwilling even to bring the subject up He could hardly blame her. After all, things weren't exactly going the way either of them had planned. Whatever enthusiasm she had about his writing was long gone. Though he was too proud to admit it, he too was beginning to doubt his ability to see the project through.

Unfortunately it was already too late for him to back out. Months before he'd managed to find a publisher, negotiate a contract and sign away his life. He had only eight months left until the deadline, the clock was ticking and his back was to the wall.

The anxiety was so overwhelming that every time he sat down to write, his mind went completely blank. Try as he might, he couldn't seem to get it together. Finally, after several more unproductive weeks of staring into a blank computer screen, he'd reached the end of his rope. His inner adult was trapped in an intellectual vortex, his inner parent was drifting aimlessly through the great existential void in search of some cosmic connection to the rest of the ectoplasmic universe and his inner child was on the verge of a full-blown tolerance break.

Visions of suicide, murder and maim filled his head. It took every bit of strength he had just to keep himself from throwing his word processor out of the window. Thrashing his computer was not a new idea, but this time he was angry enough to do it. The next thing he knew he was in a blind rage, holding his PC over his head. He was just about to let it fly when out of nowhere, his inner parent came blazing back from the void and took hold of his angry inner child.

The script below is a translation of the dialogue that went on between his inner parent, adult and child following this timely intervention:

Child to Parent: Let go of me. I've had enough of this crap. I'm going to put this piece of blankety-blank junk out of its misery. I'm tired of playing second fiddle to a computer from hell. You care more about this stupid old thing than you do about me. I quit!

Parent to Child: Okay, okay, I hear you. You're really angry, but destroying the computer is not an answer. The problem isn't the computer, it's that our inner adult and I have been so caught up in our own stuff, we've failed to be there for you. I don't blame you for being so angry. I'd feel the same way if I were you.

Child to Parent: I'm not willing to spend another day sitting in front of that stupid, ugly no-brained piece of high-tech junk.

Parent to Child: I totally agree. We need to turn the damn thing off and take some time to play. What we need to do now is go and talk to the adult. I know I can get him to see the wisdom of what you're saying.

Child to Parent: You mean you're not going to give me one of those long-winded sermons about how fortunate I am and how grateful I ought to be for all the things we have?

Parent to Child: No, I'm not going to preach to you. What I'm going to do is start taking better care of you.

Child to Parent: I don't know if I believe you. You've been acting like you're not even there and that really scares me.

Parent to Child: It does look that way, doesn't it? Well, I'm back now and I'm going to see that things get back on the right track. The adult and I both need to get with the program. Believe it or not, I want you to know that I love you and I'm sorry. What this family needs to do is sit down together and have a good old-fashioned heart-to-heart.

Parent to Adult: Excuse me, Mr. Know-It-All, but our inner child and I would like to have a few words with you, if you don't mind.

Child to Adult: Yeah, we want to talk to you about what's going on here.

Adult to Both: All right, I'm listening. What's on your mind?

Parent to Adult: Well, to start with, we need to let you know that we're both angry about how obsessed you've become about this book. It's just not right!

Adult to Parent: Not right, look who's talking! You haven't exactly been doing such a great job yourself. At least I've been trying to do what needed to get done. I thought you were the one who was supposed to be taking care of our kid.

Parent to Adult: You're right, I haven't been doing my job either. But now I realize that it's you and I together who are the problem.

Adult to Parent: So what are you suggesting we do?

Parent to Adult: Well, to start with, I suggest that we take a three-day break from all this and give it a rest.

Child to Adult: Yeah, let's go have some fun. See a movie, go out to dinner with the wife, visit some friends and maybe even sleep in for a change. We haven't done anything fun for four months.

Parent to Adult: He's right, you know, we haven't had any fun and I think it's time we did.

Adult to Parent: What about the book? We do have a deadline to meet, you know.

Parent to Adult: I know about the deadline, but it's not as though we're getting anywhere this way, are we?

Adult to Parent: No, I suppose not, God knows I've been wanting to take a break. I think you guys are right. We all need to take a break and give ourselves a chance to clean out our pipes.

Child to Parent: Does this mean we're going to go out and play?

Parent to Child: Yes, sir, that's exactly what it means.

Child: All right, let's go.

Adult: You bet, let's go. After all, there's really no choice. We can sit here and waste three more days in front of this blasted machine, or we can go and spend three fun-filled days having fun with our wife.

Parent: Well, that makes it unanimous. Let's party!

So the man went to his wife and told her that he felt it would be a good idea if he backed off the book for a while. He told her that he felt bad about all the time she had had to spend alone and asked her if she would like to spend the next few days just playing together.

His sudden interest in doing something other than writing came as somewhat of a surprise. She didn't know what to say to him, so she told him that she'd have to think about it before she could give him an answer. He understood what she was saying and left the room.

Below is a transcript of what she had to say to herself about his offer.

Child to Parent: I don't trust this. We haven't done anything fun with him for so long that I don't even know if I remember how. The whole idea scares me. Besides, he hasn't paid much attention to us up to now, so why should we worry about what he wants? I'm really mad at him and I don't know if I'm ready to let go of my anger yet. He's abandoned me plenty. Maybe we should give him a dose of his own medicine and see how he likes it.

Parent to Child: I can see that you're really angry with him.

Child to Parent: Yeah, I am and I'm going to let him have it!

Parent to Child: I know, it really hurts when your best friend doesn't have any time for you. Nobody likes being abandoned. It's hard to be patient and share your time.

Child to Parent: Patient! This has been going on now for a year. And as for sharing, I've shared all I'm going to. None of this is turning out like you promised it would. What about me?

Parent to Child: You're right, it hasn't gone the way any of us thought. Still, we did all agree to do it.

Child to Parent: No way, I didn't agree. It was you and the adult who decided that this book had to be written. I could have cared less!

Parent to Child: That's right. It wasn't really your decision, it was ours. All I can tell you is that we did try to take your feelings into account and that we did what we thought was best for all of us. It just didn't turn out as we'd hoped. There must be something we can do to make good of all this.

Adult: I've been listening to the conversation you two are having and several things occur to me. The first thing is that we don't need him to have a good time. We know how to do that by ourselves. Second, it's not just an issue of how the book has affected us, it's a matter of how it's affected all the other parts of our life — things like our kids, the finances and the house. Third, his offer gives us an opportunity to renegotiate this whole deal. And finally, we should table the discussion of our weekend together with him until we get these other issues resolved. Logically, that's the way I see it.

Parent to Adult: Makes good sense to me. I think it's only right and fair that we do this.

Parent to Child: So, how do you feel about that?

Child: It sounds really scary to me. What if he gets mad?

Adult to Child: Don't worry, kid, your parent and I are in charge. We'll take care of you. No matter what the outcome, we promise that we're going to have some fun.

Parent to Child: Absolutely. We're going to have some fun, no matter what.

The point of these two intrapersonal dialogues is to give you a firsthand look at the healthy transactional process of the inner family. These two examples demonstrate how a circular model of communication can be used to bring about an honest, respectful and loving resolution to the various conflicts of our intrapersonal family.

As you read through each dialogue again, note how all three dimensions of the inner family were involved in the process and how each was allowed to voice his/her own thoughts and feelings. Also note how, in both cases, the inner adult and parent abstained from guilting or shaming the inner child. Finally, take note of the fact that in neither case was the inner child called upon to make the decisions.

Choreographed as these two intrapersonal conversations might seem, I assure you they are not. I know, because I took them verbatim from two individuals with whom I am intimately involved, namely myself and my wife Anne. Though edited down, both the story line and dialogue represent a factual recounting of the events that took place during the writing of my first book, *Lost in the Shuffle*.

Fortunately Anne and I had progressed to a point in our individual recoveries that we were able to resolve the intrapersonal dimensions of this conflict. Eventually the culmination of our efforts would lead to the healthy interpersonal conversation shown in Figure 17.1.

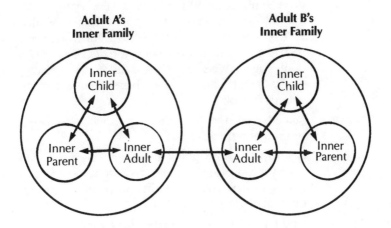

Figure 17.1. Adult-To-Adult Communication

Wife: Before I can decide about the weekend, there are some issues I want to discuss with you about this book. Is now a convenient time for you?

Husband: Sure, if you want to.

Wife: To begin with, I need you to know that I'm still committed to helping you through this project and that I believe it's important to you. I know that we agreed to your doing this book, but it's clearly turned out to be much more of an ordeal than either of us could have imagined. What a prophetic title! I feel like the one who's lost in the shuffle.

Husband: I don't mean to laugh, but what you're saying is really true, I feel the same way.

Wife: I would think so. The issue for me isn't whether you should write this book, but the amount of time that it consumes. Add to this all the travel and counseling you do, and it leaves very little time for me, the children or the things that need to be done around the house. I think what's missing here is balance.

Husband: I don't like hearing it, but I know you're absolutely right. I haven't been able to fit it all in.

Wife: That's just the point! You're trying to do too much. I don't think, given all the things you're trying to do, that any one person could do it all. I realize now that we're stuck with this deadline, so I guess we'll just have to persevere. But I'm telling you right now I won't do this again. When this book is finished, we need to sit down and come up with a better plan for writing your next book.

Husband: Agreed. I need to organize things a whole lot better before I ever try this again.

Wife: Neither of us knew going into it how much time and energy it was going to take. Obviously we do now, and I want to make darn sure that we never have to go through this again.

Husband: God knows, it hasn't been a picnic for any of us, and quite frankly I don't think I could face having to write another book if this is the way it has to be. The worst part for me has been trying to deal with all the guilt I feel over not being there for you and the kids. I know it isn't fair that you have all had to suffer through this with me.
I feel better just talking about it with you, but what really feels good is the idea of sitting down together and working out a better plan for the next time around.

Wife: Okay, since we both agree that we're not going to do it this way again and that there is little we can do to change the situation now, I think getting away for the weekend would do a lot of good to help alleviate our stress. So let's do that and forget about this book for the next three days.

Husband: Great. I'm lucky I've got you in my life. It would be a lonely trip without you. I love you, Anne.

Wife: I love you too. I've missed being with you and I am looking forward to the weekend.

This kind of healthy interpersonal conversation was not something that came easily to Anne and me. It was something that we had to work on. It doesn't always go so well, but then nothing's perfect. The thing that has helped us most over our ten years together has been the knowledge that our love, commitment and future all depend on our willingness to be there for ourselves. In other words our relationship to each other comes second to our relationship to ourselves. The concepts of identity, intimacy, commitment and love all depend on this one basic principle.

Today Anne and I face one another as adults who are not looking, as we did before, for someone else to give us the love that we need to give to ourselves. "Love thy neighbor as thyself" means just that: Learn to love yourself and you also will learn how to love your neighbor.

This is not just some Pollyanna notion, but rather a healthy prescription for living. It's a wonderful paradox — the more we come to know and love ourselves, the more we will come to know and love others. From this healthy vantage point one might even come to think of selfishness as a good thing. I do.

The Signs On The Road
To Recovery:
A Brief Review

The road to recovery is not a straight and smooth path. We need all the help we can get on our journey. This final chapter is designed to be used as a reference — a few signs on the road to remind you where you've been, where you are and where you're going.

The blank pages at the end of the book are for your use as personal work sheets. Please use them to complete some of the exercises suggested in this book, such as making a list of your family rules and mapping your family within. Your personal record will be another sign on the road that tells you just how far you have come. Use them — you'll be surprised at how far you've come.

Bon voyage!

Reviewing The Facts

Fact 1: Our inner child is innocent and not responsible for the ignorance and lack of direction of our inner parent and adult. He or she is the emotionally baffling dimension of co-dependency.

Fact 2: Our inner child will always remain a child. He or she is the emotional and intuitive copilot of our inner family. Our inner child is a reservoir of strength and our best link to all that is good and divine in the world.

Fact 3: Our inner parent is the moral and ethical guide of our inner family. He/she is responsible for the physical, emotional and psychological well-being of our inner child. Our inner parent is literally our conscience and keeper of the faith. She/he is the powerful dimension of our inner family.

Fact 4: Our inner adult is the cognitive, rational and intellectual side of our spirit, that logical and cunning dimension of our inner family whose job it is to listen for the moral and emotional direction of our inner parent and child. In the metaphorical sense, our inner adult is the one who should always be sitting behind the wheel of our bus.

Fact 5: No one dimension of the inner family is more important than the other. Each needs to be seen as separate, but equal.

Fact 6: Co-dependency is a dis-ease of the intrapersonal spirit. It is characterized by a physical, emotional and psychological pattern of coping that is caused by the practice of, or adherence to, a set of dysfunctional family rules. In clinical terms co-dependency is a delayed identity development syndrome.

Fact 7: There are six primary stages of psycho-emotional development:
1. Trust *versus* Mistrust (birth – 18 months)
2. Autonomy *versus* Shame and Doubt (12 months – 3 years)
3. Initiative *versus* Guilt (2 – 6 years)
4. Industry *versus* Inferiority (4 – 16 years)
5. Identity *versus* Identity Confusion (14 – 25 years)
6. Intimacy *versus* Isolation (16 years – death)

Fact 8: Identity orientation is different for men and women. A man's identity tends to be more focused on an intrapersonal basis, while a woman's identity tends to be more focused on an interpersonal basis. In a co-dependent culture like ours, the male identity is built primarily on a work-ethic mentality, while the female identity is built primarily on a relationship ethic.

Fact 9: Sex and intimacy are mutually exclusive. Sometimes they happen together; but having sex does not necessarily mean having intimacy. Intimacy is the process of sharing openly and honestly within yourself or with others. Sex is the process of sharing physically with self or others.

Fact 10: *Guilt* is the feeling we get when we think that we've made a mistake. *Shame* is the feeling we get when we think that we *are* a mistake.

Unhealthy guilt stems from the dysfunctional rules of our inner adult. Shame stems from the dysfunctional expectations of our inner parent.
Unhealthy guilt + shame = shilt.

Fact 11: Identity means having a clear, open, honest and loving relationship with oneself. Intimacy means having a clear, open, honest and loving relationship with self and/or others. Together these two components of relationship — identity and intimacy — translate into dimensions of spirituality, which means relationship.

Fact 12: In order to recover from co-dependency and heal the family within we must break out of a rigid hierarchical model of the inner family and move toward a circular model of the inner family. Visually this means changing the structure of the intrapersonal family, as shown in Figure 18.1.

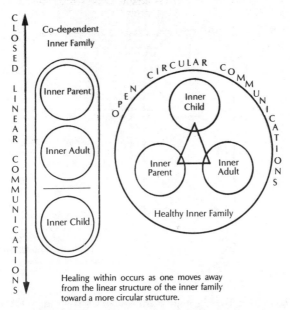

Healing within occurs as one moves away from the linear structure of the inner family toward a more circular structure.

Figure 18.1. From Co-dependency To Health

Who? What? How? And Why?

Who?

- *Who is the logical overseer of the intrapersonal family?* The inner adult.
- *Who is the governor of our morality and keeper of the faith?* Our inner parent.
- *Who is the reservoir of our emotional and intuitive wisdom?* The inner child.
- *Who is the cunning dimension of our inner family?* The inner adult.
- *Who is the powerful dimension of our inner family?* The inner parent.
- *Who is the baffling dimension of our inner family?* The inner child.
- *Who should be driving our bus?* The inner adult.
- *Who should be the primary caretaker of our inner child?* The inner parent.
- *Who should be guided by, but free of, intellectual and moral responsibility?* The inner child.

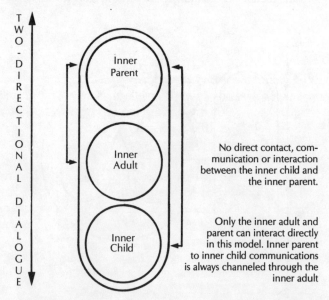

Figure 18.2. The Co-dependent Model Of The Family Within

What?

- *What is the development order of the inner family?* First, the inner child; second, the inner adult and third, the inner parent.
- *What does the co-dependent structure of the inner family look like?* Linear and hierarchical, with only two-directional communications possible (see Figure 18.2).
- *What does the structure of the healthy intrapersonal family look like?* Balanced and circular allowing for the open communication and interaction between all three dimensions of the inner family (see Figure 18.3).

How?

- *How many potential famlies are there within the linear co-dependent model of the inner family?* Three. The inner parent, adult and child; the inner parent and adult; and the inner adult and child (see Figure 18.4).
- *How many potential families are there in the healthy circular model of the inner family?* Four: The inner parent, adult and child; the inner parent and adult; the inner parent and child and the inner adult and child (see Figure 18.5).

Why?

- *Why should the inner adult always drive?* Because it is our inner adult who possesses the intellectual and cognitive ability to reason objectively through the emotional and moral dimensions of our inner child and parent. The inner child is our emotional barometer; and the inner parent is our moral barometer. Ideally the inner parent and child should serve as copilots and consultants to the inner adult. In a healthy model of the intrapersonal family, the inner adult is capable of three-dimensional logic. That is, he or she is competent to integrate the principles of pure logic, moral logic and emotional logic into the decision-making process.
- *Why is our inner child innocent?* Because he/she is not competent to sort through the intellectual and moral dimensions of an adult reality. Our inner child is an emotional and intuitive creature who, like all children, will tend toward over-reaction or under-reaction if left unattended.

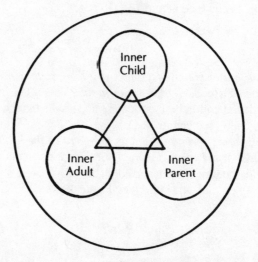

In the healthy circular model no one member is more important than
another. The circular model is not rigid but fluid. Communication and
interaction is open between all three dimensions. There is no fixed
positioning of the inner parent, adult or child within this model. Identity, intimacy and spirituality are all parts of a unified intrapersonal
family.

Figure 18.3. The Healthy Circular Model Of The Family Within

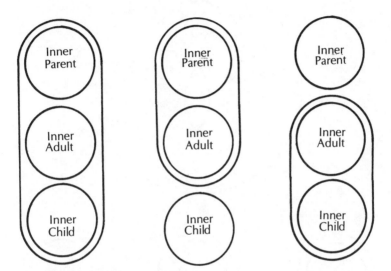

These three intrapersonal family relationships that exist within the co-dependent structure tend to be uncooperative, antagonistic and counterproductive. This is due primarily to the dysfunctional co-dependent rules that restrict and undermine developmental growth of the family as a whole. This in turn creates a delayed identity development syndrome and a need to seek from the outside that which is missing on the inside — like a loving parent, for example.

Figure 18.4. Potential Families Within The Co-dependent Structure Of The Family Within

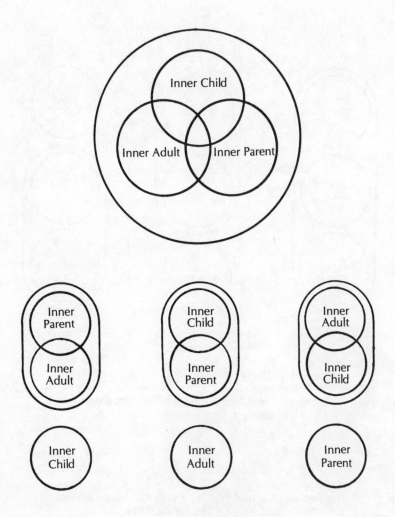

**Figure 18.5. Potential Families Within The Healthy
Structure Of The Family Within**

- *Why do we feel guilt?* Because we believe that we have done something wrong.
- *Why do we feel shame?* Because we believe that we are wrong.
- *Why do we lack a clear sense of identity?* Because we have not yet resolved many of the developmental conflicts from our childhood, such as basic trust, autonomy, initiative and industry.
- *Why do adult child/co-dependents have problems being intimate with others?* Because they lack a clear identity and sense of intimacy within themselves.
- *Why is it so difficult to heal our family within?* Because our inner parent and adult continue to operate as though they are victims rather than volunteers and because they continue to live under a set of dysfunctional family rules.
- *Why are you reading this book?* Because, like me, you are searching for answers. And because, like me, you deserve to be happy.

Well, folks, that is about it. I've come as far I can. The rest is up to you. My wish for you now is that you trust in the process, seek out the help you need, discover your hidden potential and heal your family within.

There are many roads to the top of the mountain, but only one path that is right for you. So listen to your inner child and trust that she or he will know the right path for you to follow.

From My Inner Family
To Yours

There is no sure or clear-cut way.
Our healing comes, but day by day.

No hope is there to heal the skin
that has no strength or life within.

But hope have I that you will find
the life you wish as I found mine.

If with yourself you dare to be
I know you'll find your family three.

Between them lies the promised land
One Self, One Grace, One Loving Hand.

Reference Notes

2. In The Beginning
"Counselor in," in Dr. Douglas Talbott

3. Just Another Day in Court
If you have, **Alcoholics Anonymous** 58-59.
I think that . . . in bright sunshine, Bill Wilson, "Emotional Recovery," *The Grapevine* (January 1958)

4. The Co-dependent Dimension
"Recovery is not," Peg Subby, *Pieces of Silence: The Family Legacy of Alcoholism and Co-dependency* (Video, 1979).

5. Changing From The Inside Out
1. Trust . . . Isolation, E.H. Erikson, "Identity and the Life Cycle," *Psychological Issues* No. 1 (New York: International Universities Press, 1959).
The manner in Jacob L. Orlofsky, Ph.D., **The Relationship Between Intimacy Status and Antecedent Personality Components.**

The depth of David Morris, "Attachment and Intimacy," in **Intimacy**, edited by Martin Fisher and George Stricker (Plenum Press, 1982).

children are not, *Ibid.*

leads to an . . . significant others, *Ibid.,* 313.

6. Understanding Identity

Allen Sroufe, and David Morris, "Attachment and Intimacy," in *Intimacy,* edited by Martin Fisher and George Stricker (Plenum Press, 1982).

despite Erikson's presentation *Ibid.,* 319.

the capacity to, E.H. Erikson, **Childhood and Society**, 2d ed. (New York: Norton, 1963), 203.

Failure at this, Jacob L. Orlofsky, Ph.D., *Adolescence XIII,* no. 51 (Fall 1978):.

secure base . . . oversensitive Morris, **Intimacy**.

He may be, *Ibid.,* 314.

a person's psychological, Virginia Satir, **Conjoint Family Therapy** (Palo Alto, CA: Science & Behavior, 1967).

the blurring of Satir in Morris, **Intimacy**.

the dependent belief, Morris **Intimacy**, 318

isolation, stereotyped relations, E.H. Erikson, "Identity and the Life Cycle," *Psychological Issues* No. 1 (New York: International Universities Press, 1959), 125.

A dependent person Bowlby, in Morris, **Intimacy**, 319.

more dysfunctional people *Ibid.,* 319.

9. Four Faces of Identity

identity states, The information on the four states of identity in this chapter is drawn on Friel, Friel, and Robert Subby, **Co-dependency and the Search for Identity** (Hollywood, FL: Health Communications, 1984), 5-12.

11. Dimensions of the Spirit

The cordial relationship, Eric Berne.

Figures 11.2 and 11.3 from **Current Psychologies.**

Other Materials By Robert Subby

HEALING THE FAMILY WITHIN (Video)
Code 4119V . . . . (44 min.) $275.00

LOST IN THE SHUFFLE: The Co-dependent Reality
Best-Seller
Robert Subby

Robert Subby defines the condition of co-dependency, the problems, the pitfalls, the unreal rules the co-dependent lives by, and the way out of the dis-eased condition to recovery.
ISBN 0-932194-45-1 . . . . $8.95
Audio book available. ISBN 0-932194-92-3 . . . . $8.95

PIECES OF SILENCE
Robert Subby

This is the story of a family that has suffered the effects of having an alcoholic parent. Personal interviews with the Subby family illustrate the pain, guilt and frustration of growing up in a dysfunctional family with an alcoholic parent.
Code 4105V . . . . (½″ VHS, 60 min.) $275.00

CO-DEPENDENCY AND FAMILY RULES
Robert Subby and John Friel

This pamphlet clearly defines co-dependency as a dysfunctional pattern of living and problem-solving, which is nurtured by a set of rules within the family system.
Code 2132 . . . . (Pamphlet) . . . . $.75

**CO-DEPENDENCY AND THE
SEARCH FOR IDENTITY**
Robert Subby, John Friel and Linda Friel

This pamphlet was the first in the co-dependency series and relates issues of self-esteem and identification of feelings in adults to the patterns developed in the systems of a dysfunctional family.
Code 2141 . . . . (Pamphlet) . . . . $.75